Buying a Home:

Don't Let Them Make a Monkey Out of You

By Alysse Musgrave

2

For Richard and Lia, the loves of my life

In loving Memory of Dean Moye'

Table of Contents

About the Author

Alysse Musgrave is a graduate of Texas A&M University, and has been a licensed real estate broker in the state of Texas since 1995. While working as a systems analyst, she developed an interest in flipping houses and earned her real estate license to support her personal investment efforts.

Learning firsthand of the pitfalls and negative aspects of buying and selling real estate, Alysse developed an empathy for others who experienced her frustration. Especially discouraged by the lack of representation she received as a buyer, Alysse decided the time was right to bring Exclusive Buyer Agency to the Dallas/Ft. Worth area, and she opened what would become one of Dallas' oldest and most successful exclusive buyer brokerages.

In writing this book, Alysse hopes to provide those entering the often frightening world of the homebuyer with a resource to empower and enlighten and make finding the perfect home one of life's positive experiences.

Introduction

Let's face it. In a real estate transaction the buyer assumes all of the risk. The seller walks away from the property and is free of any obligation or responsibility. The buyer pays for inspections, appraisals, closing costs, and ends up with the house and a mortgage. At best, buying a home is a complicated process. At worst, it can be an emotional and financial nightmare. Not only do you have to find a house that you love, you have to verify its condition, negotiate a good price, figure out how to pay for it, insure it, move in, all the while ensuring you are buying a home that you will be able to resell for a profit when the time comes. The list of things to consider is seemingly endless.

Before 1989, all real estate agents worked for the seller and these agents were not required to disclose this fact to the buyer. The agent would spend many days in the car with a potential buyer, and that buyer had no idea that the agent had a fiduciary duty to tell the seller everything the buyer said. If the buyer offered $400,000 for a house but stated that they would be willing to go up to $450,000, the agent was required by law to pass that information along to the seller.

As expected, lawsuits were filed across the country when buyers learned that they could have purchased property for a lot less money, had they known whom the agent represented. As a result, most states implemented disclosure requirements. At the first meeting with a potential buyer or seller, agents were required to disclose which party they represented. Most states implemented policies and procedures that gave the *illusion* of fairness, but one thing remained the same: The buyer still assumed the risk and the buyer is still the target of most of the fraud.

Exclusive Buyer Agency was born in 1989, finally providing the buyer with the opportunity to buy a home with the same level of representation that sellers have always enjoyed. But, since there are relatively few agents who work with buyers exclusively, most buyers are forced to accept substandard representation.

The real estate system in this country is broken, and there is no easy fix. In a perfect world, each party to the transaction would pay for their own representation. Commissions would be fixed since it is no more work to help someone buy a $600,000 house than it is to help them buy a $100,000 house. However, buyers do not want to pay to pay their own agent because they need their cash for their closing costs, and traditional real estate brokerages are not going to cut profits and change tried and true business models voluntarily, so here the issue lies. Buyers have to learn to navigate through a homebuying process in which mortgage fraud runs rampant and buyers very rarely have proper representation.

My goal in writing this book is not to teach the reader everything there is to know about buying a home; there are thousands of variables, and real estate law varies from state to state. My goal is to share information with the reader that will help them make good choices, and will help them recognize fraud when they see it.

So who am I? My name is Alysse Musgrave, and I am the broker and owner of one of the oldest and most successful exclusive buyer brokerages in the country. Since 1995, I have been protecting the rights of homebuyers, speaking out against predatory lending practices, and have saved my clients thousands and thousands of dollars. I am one of a relatively few number of exclusive buyer brokers in this country, and we are all committed to the same cause: to keep homebuyers from getting ripped off.

In the pages that follow, I'll share with readers all the information I share with my own clients, and hopefully my words and advice will lead to a seamless and stress-free homebuying experience, and years of comfort and financial happiness in their new home!

About this Book

It's been said that a good non-fiction book conveys to the reader only the necessary information – and not one word more.

That's what I do in this book. I tell you only what you really need to know and I leave out all the fluff. You will notice that I did not include links to mortgage calculators or to the Department of Housing and Development's website. There isn't a glossary with the definitions of a thousand words you really don't need, or care, to know.

In this book, I strive to teach you things that no other Realtor will tell you. You will learn how to recognize a good floor plan, how to negotiate with the seller, how to get the information you really need from your loan officer, and much more.

As a thank you for buying this book, I'd like you to feel welcome to contact me at Help@HelpUBuyAmerica.com with any questions you may have, and to tell me about your homebuying experience. I hope it will be a good one. And, if you find this book useful, please take the time to write a review. Amazon, Barnes & Noble, iBook, and all the others, are wonderful platforms that will allow me to disseminate truly useful information to buyers across the country. It is my hope that no homebuyer will ever be ripped off again!

CHAPTER ONE
Real Estate Agents

Do I Need a Real Estate Agent

A real estate agent is a person who is licensed to list and sell real estate; a Realtor is a real estate agent who is also a member of the National Association of Realtors. A Realtor is always a real estate agent, but not every real estate agent is a Realtor. In this book, I use the terms "agent" and "Realtor" interchangeably.

People have come to assume that Realtors have no value, especially since the MLS (Multiple Listing Service), the database of homes for sale, has become accessible to anyone with a computer and online access. It doesn't help that Realtors in general rank just below car salesmen in likeability and trustworthiness. However, the truth is that a good real estate agent can save you tens of thousands of dollars and substantially reduce the risks involved with purchasing a home.

Searching the MLS for a home is something you can do on your own. To get inside the house you need an agent. Even monkeys, however, can open a door to a house. A Realtor's value lies in his or her knowledge of pricing, marketing, marketability, finance, homeowner's insurance, title insurance, surveys, and especially in the individual's ability to negotiate a great price and protect your rights as a homebuyer.

Most agents will tell you that it took 7-10 transactions before they felt 100 percent comfortable with the process. To think you can buy a home without an agent simply because you read this book, or "Homebuying for Dummies," is a mistake. You need an agent or a lawyer, and in some states, you need both.

Types of Agents

It is important that the agent you hire is a full-time, career agent. It benefits you to work with a Realtor who makes his or her living working in real estate. Your cousin's mother-in-law who sells one or two homes a year may not be qualified to protect you. You want a full-time, well-respected, experienced Realtor. Next, you need the right type of representation. The names vary state by state, but, essentially, the following types of agents are the agents with which you should be familiar: Exclusive buyer agents, buyer agents, dual agents, seller agents, real estate consultants, and discounters. In the following sections, I will describe the roles of these agents.

Exclusive Buyer Agents

An Exclusive Buyer Agent works in an office that never takes listings and never represents sellers. It's all buyers, all the time. There is absolutely no conflict of interest that could jeopardize your negotiating position. For a buyer, EBAs are the Mercedes Benz of representation.

Buyer Agents

Buyer agents work for companies that represent both buyers and sellers (Re/Max, Keller Williams, Ebby, Century 21, etc.). There are incentives and pressure for these agents to try to sell in-house listings, so they essentially are not working for the buyer, even if they claim otherwise. If your Re/Max agent shows you a home listed by someone in their office and you decide you want to buy it, the office has procedures to "represent" both sides of the transaction. These types of offices tend to favor the seller more than the buyer, as evidenced by all the ads telling you how much they have "sold." As a buyer, you are not looking to be "sold," you want to "save" and not get ripped off!

Dual Agents

A dual agent is one that works for the buyer and the seller in the same transaction. Technically, dual agency is not legal in Texas and many other states, but there is always a way around the law that works against both sellers and buyers, and it is still quite difficult to tell the difference between a "buyer agent" and a "dual agent", or a "seller agent" and a "dual agent." Should a Texas Realtor wish tosell a seller/client's house to one of their buyer/clients, they use a third party *in their office* to handle negotiations for one of the parties, to the detriment of everyone except the broker.

20

The following is an example to illustrate what it is like to work with a dual agent. Suppose you drive by a house that interests you and notice that there is a Century 21 sign in the yard. You decide to call the number printed on the sign, and a very nice Realtor answers the call. This Realtor was hired by the owners of the house to sell their property and get them as much money as possible. On the phone, the Realtor offers to show you the house, so you set up a time to meet and view her listing. You like the house but are not ready to commit, so the Realtor offers to show you some other homes that you might like. While looking at the first house, the Realtor represented the seller. Now they are showing you other agent's listings in which they would represent you as a buyer's agent, should you opt to buy one of those homes. In the meantime, they've asked you all kinds of questions and has a clear picture of your purchasing power and the level of your motivation. If you decide to buy the first house they showed you (or any of their other listings) they'd have to turn you over to someone else in their office, but would be legally obligated to tell their seller/client everything they knows about you. And, from the seller's standpoint, the agent used their house as a source of buyer leads. The seller most likely shared all of their secrets with this agent, only to have that information used against them if both the buyer side and seller side of the transaction are handled in-house with the same broker. It's a convoluted mess, and it is unfair to both the seller and the buyer, and the only person who wins here is the Realtor and their broker.

Seller Agents

Seller agents work in a traditional real estate office that takes listings. They market the home via advertisements and open houses. They become dual agents when they represent the buyer. I have yet to meet an agent who only represents sellers.

Real Estate Consultant

Real estate consultants typically offer services to buyers and sellers on an a-la-carte basis, if you will. For example, instead of paying a six percent commission, a seller can pay a consultant a fixed rate to list the home on the MLS or to provide a market analysis. Buyers can pay an agent a fee just to write the purchase contract or to show them a specific home. This is a great way, in my opinion, for real estate to be bought and sold, and some Realtors are beginning to offer consulting services. Currently these services are more beneficial to the sellers than for buyers, but hopefully that will change.

Discounters

Most Realtors detest the idea of discounting their commission; I don't. I think if a buyer can do some of the legwork, they are entitled to part of the commission. Most, but not all, discounters are rebating commissions because they can't compete with other agents in their area. Or, they are online only brokers that you never meet, and they never see the house you are buying; they only serve to write the contracts. My advice is to stay away from these types. If you can find a busy, career agent who will reduce his or her commission by offering a reduced level of service, but will still offer you advice and guidance, it can be a great way to buy a house.

How Agents Get Paid

When a homeowner decides to sell a home, they typically hire a traditional Realtor who works with both buyers and sellers. Commissions are negotiable but are typically 5-7 percent of the sale price. The Realtor lists the home on the MLS, and by doing so agrees to split the commission with the agent who brings a qualified buyer. At closing, the seller's proceeds are reduced in the amount of the negotiated commission. That amount is split between the buyer's agent and the seller's agent. Some buyers believe that they can get a better price for a home if no Realtor is involved, and sometimes that is true. The seller might be willing to sell the house for less if they do not have to pay Realtor fees, or they may choose to maximize their own profits.

How to Find a Great Agent

To find an exclusive buyer agent visit www.NAEBA.org. However, since less than half of one percent of real estate agents are EBAs, you may not be able to find one to work with you. If this is the case, you may be forced to work with a traditional agent that represents both buyers and sellers. Find an agent with whom you feel comfortable, but don't share too much information! You never know when they are going to switch to the other side. If they have a listing in your price range, they are almost certainly going to show it to you, since this will allow them to earn both sides of the commission. It is wise to refrain from telling them anything that could be used against you later! The buyer's negotiating position is highly compromised in this type of office, and a truly level playing field only exists when the buyer works with an EBA. Share what you must, but keep your secrets to yourself! That means do not share information such as how much you can afford, and do not appear too anxious when you find a home you like. Treat the Realtor as a friendly adversary, not as someone you can trust with your money.

Interviewing Agents

Even if your best friend recommended an agent to you, you should at the very least meet the agent before you start to look at houses. The agent/buyer relationship can be a long one, and the two personalities need to "click," to a certain degree. Imagine spending weeks looking at homes with someone you don't like! Here are some questions you need to ask prospective agents:

How long have you been in business?

Because the buyer assumes the risk in a real estate transaction, you need an agent with at least 3-5 years experience.

Are you a full-time Realtor?

Your agent absolutely must be a full-time career agent. He or she should be available to show you homes during normal business hours, not only on nights and weekends.

Who do you represent?

Most agents will state that they represent both buyers and sellers, and some will state that even though they work in a traditional real estate office that takes listings, *they* only work with buyers, or that they are their office's buyer specialist. The truth is that it doesn't matter what they say; if they are not an EBA, they represent both sides. It is imperative that I make this point clear.

How do you handle competing buyers?

What happens if the agent has a buyer who is looking for the same type of house as one of their other buyers? Who gets the first look at the property, and what happens if both buyers want to make an offer? This is an area of concern for me. My personal policy is that I don't take on two clients looking for exactly the same property.

How do you handle in-house listings?

There are incentives for Re/Max agents, for example, to show Re/Max listed homes. How do they handle representing both the buyer and seller in the same transaction? Are you going to be turned over to another agent to handle your negotiations? Know their procedures.

How will you notify me of new listings?

In my office, we use the Home Finder Service, which automatically sends new listings to my clients each day. Clients can go online and look at pictures, take virtual tours, and make notes about homes they like. It helps us communicate about specific homes and to stay organized.

How much notice do you need for appointments?

A successful career agent isn't going to be available at the drop of a hat to show you a home. I schedule my weekend showings five or six days in advance but am often more flexible during the week. I also have an assistant who can show a home for me in case of emergency. Find out how your prospective agent works.

How do you get paid?

Commissions are negotiable but most residential buyer agents work for three percent of the sales price, and the fee is deducted from the seller's proceeds at closing. Some Realtors charge buyers an upfront retainer, which is fully refundable at closing. Realtors often use retainers to eliminate buyers who are time wasters. I personally collect a small deposit but there are many agents who will be inexperienced or desperate enough to drive you around and show you houses for free.

Can I review copies of your paperwork?

Don't feel pressured into signing a buyer's representation agreement on the spot. Take it home, review it, and negotiate the terms with which you don't agree.

What happens to bonuses that are offered to the selling agent?

If the sellers are offering to pay a $5,000 bonus to the agent who brings them a buyer, what happens to this money? Some agents will state that they can keep the bonus as long as it is disclosed to all parties. Don't trust this agent! Our policy is to rebate all bonuses and money in excess of the negotiated commission back to the buyer. That should be your policy too.

What happens if the seller only offers two percent to the buyer's agent, but yours works for three percent?

This happens sometimes with bank owned properties or sellers who have little equity in their home. Are you willing to pay your agent the extra one percent by rolling it into the price of the home? Or will you pay the agent in cash? If not, do you want your agent to even show you homes that offer less than a three percent commission? This is an important issue and you would do well to make your wishes known.

Meaningless Questions

You can ask the following questions, if you like, but don't put too much stock in their answers.

Do you have references?

All agents have references but it doesn't necessarily mean they are meaningful or even real. Even the reviews you read online aren't necessarily accurate. You need to visit the website of the real estate commission in your state to see if they have been disciplined for any reason. Get a referral from a friend if you can, but always have an exit strategy or a plan to end the relationship if it is not working out.

Can the agent give me a list of buyer clients with their addresses and how much they saved?

An agent who would give you this information is not very smart. I would never compromise my client's safety and privacy in order to get a new client. New homeowners become the target of many, many scams, and I'm not going to inadvertently become part of a transaction that harms my clients. Find an agent who has integrity and concern for things other than their own pocketbook.

How much of a discount can you usually get off the price of a home?

There are far too many variables for anyone to be able to answer this question accurately, and any answer you receive would be a complete guess or a total lie. Price is only one of many possible seller concessions. And, if five buyers are competing for the same house, you want the agent that is going to be able to convince the seller's side to sell the house to you, not one of the other four buyers. You need an agent who can present your offer in a way that wins you the house, and often, it has nothing to do with money.

Buyer Representation Agreements

A buyer's representation agreement is an employment contract that spells out the duties and responsibilities of the Realtor to the buyer, and vice versa. Most Realtors will want you to sign one. In fact, some won't show you a home until they have you under contract. Realtors want to ensure they will be paid for the work that they do, and it is unfair for a buyer to use their services to show houses only to switch Realtors or buy the home through a discounter at the last minute. Buyers, however, do not want to be committed to an agent, in case they decide he or she isn't doing a good job for them. Your relationship with your agent needs to make both parties comfortable. You need to feel comfortable with your agent's knowledge and responsiveness, and they need to feel comfortable with your loyalty. Do not be afraid, however, to dictate the terms of this agreement. Here are some ways you can tweak your contract with your agent:

- Instead of committing to a six-month agreement, adopt a one-month agreement with an option to renew at a later time. This will give you some time to get to know your agent before making a long-term commitment to them.

- Have the commitment apply only to the houses that they show you, and omit any mention of a time period.

- Designate a trial period, after which the full agreement goes into effect unless either party terminates the agreement.

- Most importantly, always insist on an "out" clause so that you can be released at any time. The agent will only be paid on homes that they have shown you. A good agent is going to have some sort of customer satisfaction guarantee. If they don't, find someone else.

I personally don't use this type of buyer's representation agreement. I'm confident in my skills. If a buyer/client doesn't want to work with me, they are free to go at any time with no strings attached. Working with me should be the least stressful part of the homebuying process.

If it's not working out

If you begin to work with an agent and find that it's not a good fit, you are not stuck. Don't be intimidated by a buyer's representation agreement. Before you fire them, first make sure your expectations are reasonable. Your agent isn't your companion or tour guide; their job is to help you buy a house, not to take you to lunch. Don't expect them to drop everything and show you a house at the last minute. Show up on time for all appointments, since appointments have to be made with the sellers, and do not expect calls to be returned at all hours of the night. If you are behaving this way, chances are your agent will be more than happy to release you.

If your agent hasn't shown you houses in a couple of weeks, ask why. It is possible that your search criterion is too narrow and that there is nothing to show. Agents deserve the opportunity to explain themselves, and it is easier to give them a chance than it is to start over with a new agent. If you have expressed your concerns to the agent and you are still unhappy, it's time to fire them.

How to Fire Your Agent

If your agent has shown you a home that you wish to buy but you really don't want to work them any longer, contact their broker (boss) and ask to have another agent assigned to you. The released agent will be fairly compensated for their time when the transaction closes.

If you haven't found a house through this agent, review the agreement you signed and determine the terms of the "out" clause. You usually just have to send written notification that terminates the relationship. If there isn't such a clause, send the letter anyway to both the agent and the broker and see what happens. There is no reason to be insulting or antagonistic. Simply state that you have decided not to buy a house and wish to terminate the agreement. They cannot force you to make an offer or buy a house through them. In fact, a Realtor is not entitled to receive a commission on a transaction unless they are the "procuring cause" (instigated the transaction) of the sale, although laws do vary by state.

Be aware that if the agent shows you a house and you later buy it through a discounter or circumvent them in some other way, you will probably be sued for the agent's commission, *and you will lose.*

CHAPTER TWO
Getting Started

Get Pre-Qualified

Getting pre-qualified is the very first step in the homebuying process, and is more than likely the first requirement of any Realtor you hire. A quick call to a lender will determine your buying power, your cash on hand requirements, and suitable loan programs.

Before you call, check your credit and give the loan officer your credit score. The loan officer will ask basic questions about your income, debt, cash on hand, and employment, and will send you a pre-qualification letter that tells you the price of home you can afford. At this point, don't worry about the lender's pricing or interest rate; you will shop for rates later.

Wants Versus Needs

There is a lot to consider when shopping for a home, including location, budget, property condition, schools, resale, floor plan, potential appreciation versus depreciation, and much more. It's best to start by making a list of items that are important to you, and then ranking them in order of importance. Do this before you start to look at homes so that unimportant things, like décor, do not distract you. Following are some things to consider before you start to look at homes.

Number of bedrooms and bathrooms

The safest size single family home is a four-bedroom. For resale purposes, anyone who can fit into a three-bedroom home would fit into a four-bedroom home. The opposite is not true. A family who needs a four-bedroom home would never consider a three-bedroom home. Three bedrooms are perfectly fine if a nice selection of four bedroom homes is not available in your price range. If you do buy a three-bedroom home, it would be nice to have at least two living areas in the house, or at least a space for an office.

One or Two Story Home

There are both advantages and disadvantages to either a one-story or a two-story home. In a single-story home, the ceilings can be higher and there is no noise from people walking overhead. It is easier and safer for small children and the elderly or disabled to live on one floor, and you don't have wasted space where the stairs would go. On the down side, the yard is usually smaller due to the larger footprint of the house. There is typically less privacy and the bedrooms are often smaller.

Living in a two-story home usually means nice views from the second floor, and more separation between living spaces and bedrooms. It's safe to leave windows open on the second floor, the yard is sometimes larger, and if all the bedrooms are upstairs, you don't have to heat or cool the first floor while you are sleeping. The negatives are the noise level when people are walking on the second floor, and that stairs can be inconvenient and prohibitive if a family member becomes injured or sick.

Number of living areas

Most of my clients are very happy not to have a formal living area, opting instead for a home office. The family room is typically where everyone gathers, so make sure this space is on the larger side, and be mindful of traffic patterns once all the furniture is in place. You typically need a 3' wide walkway to move from space to space. If you have children and want them to have a separate space for their toys and friends, be sure to find a home with at least two living areas. Many people like to have a separate game room just for the kids and their mess!

Number of dining areas

Although people don't use their formal living space anymore, there is still a strong demand for a formal dining room; it is preferable to have a minimum of two eating areas. Most meals will be in the breakfast room so it is important that this space is large enough to accommodate a table and at least four chairs comfortably. If the door to the back yard is in the breakfast room, be sure that there will be room to open the door once the dinette is in place. The dining room should accommodate a minimum of six people. The only exception to this rule applies to townhomes where a single dining room is somewhat common.

Garage spaces

In most parts of the country, single-family homes almost always come with a two-car garage. You may encounter homes where the homeowners have converted the garage into living space. Be sure that the space can be converted back to a garage easily, since homes without garages are harder to sell. If you are purchasing a home in a neighborhood where most of the homes have a three-car garage, do not buy a home with a two-car garage. You want your house to blend with the other homes in the neighborhood.

Square Feet

It's smart to have a general idea of what 3000 square feet looks and feels like, but do not get too concerned about numbers. The floor plan matters more than the square footage of a house. A good floor plan can make a 2500 square foot home feel like a palace. Conversely, a 4000 square foot home can feel small if there is not enough usable space or if the design is poor. If you think you want a 3000 square foot home, let your Realtor show you homes in the 2700-3300 square foot range. You never know when a house you look at will be *the* house, even though it wasn't perfect on paper.

Age of home

If you are concerned about energy conservation and your utility bills, newer is better - by far. The cost to cool a home built in the 1980s can be triple the cost to cool the same size home built in the year 2000 or later. Improvements in the quality of insulation, windows, roof decking/radiant barriers, energy star appliances and air conditioners have substantially reduced the costs to heat and cool a home. Sacrifices are to be made, however. Older homes were typically built on bigger and sometimes more beautiful lots, and have a much different look and feel than new homes, for better or for worse. If you are not sure of your preference, I suggest that you have your agent show you a few older homes. You will know right away if older homes are something you wish to consider.

Area

Decide where you want to live before you hire an agent, but be open to any suggestions that they may have. How far are you willing to drive to get to work? Do you want to be close to downtown or are you happy in the suburbs? Schools are always an important consideration, and you should buy a home in a good school district, even if you don't have children. Find out where the good schools are and then take a ride to that area, or go online and find some homes in your price range and drive around those neighborhoods just to see how you like them. An afternoon in the car can answer a lot of questions for you.

Yard Size

A large yard generally means more maintenance. If you are not willing to do the work yourself, make sure you have the money to hire someone to take care of it for you. Generally speaking, people like a larger yard. Unless you are buying a townhouse, don't buy a house with the smallest yard in the neighborhood, because you may have a hard time selling the property. Play the averages and find a home that has an average size lot or bigger.

Price range

There is a *big* difference between how much money the bank will lend you, how much you can truly afford, and how much you should be willing to spend. Just because the bank will lend you $400,000, doesn't mean you should borrow that much. Consider the monthly cost of utilities, repairs, cleaning, maintenance, and furniture. Bankrate.com has some great mortgage calculators to help you decide how much home you can comfortably afford. Aim to buy everything you need, but just some of the things you want. There is a difference.

Property Condition

How much work are you willing to do? You might be open to making cosmetic changes like paint, carpet, etc., but it is important to know your limits. If you are going to make changes to the property before you move in, be sure that you have the money for both labor and materials, even if you plan to do the work yourself. You need to have some "oops" money set aside.

Pool

People don't always realize the work and money involved with maintaining a pool. The costs include heating, cleaning, chemicals, insurance, and there is the constant concern about the safety of your children, pets, and even the neighborhood children. If you are not 100 percent certain that you want a pool, my advice is to not get one. However, if you know for certain that you want one, it is much smarter to buy a home with a pool already installed. If you add a pool later, it is likely you will only recuperate about 50 percent of your original cost, at best, when you decide to sell the home.

Working With Your Agent

Sharing your wants and needs with your Realtor will expedite the process and save you from looking at a lot of homes that won't work for you. Your agent can then send you a list of homes that suit your needs and you can make arrangements to visit the ones that are most appealing. If your list seems very brief, your requirements may not be reasonable. But do not automatically assume that you need to increase the price. Tweak some of the other criteria, like square feet, and see what compromises may need to be made.

I like to have my buyer/clients choose the homes that interest them, at least initially. It helps me learn their likes and dislikes, allowing me the opportunity to learn what appeals to them. I am always looking at FSBOs and new construction, and I need to be able recognize my buyer's dream home when I see it. I've heard buyers complain that their Realtors were not working for them when they send them lists of homes to review. I say this is nonsense.

You and your Realtor have the same goal: To help you find your dream home. They can't find you what you want if they don't know what that is. Communicate with your Realtor and don't judge his or her ability based on this part of the process. Anyone can open a door and schedule a showing. It is that which comes after the house is found that makes a good Realtor invaluable.

MLS Listed Homes

More than likely you will receive MLS listings via email, and there will be links to view photos and to take virtual tours. Lots of agents use services that will send you new listings automatically so you will know what's new on the market in real time. My Home Finder service is an online gateway that buyers can use to sort through the listings and communicate with me about the homes that appeal to them. I strongly suggest that you hire an agent who takes advantage of all the available technology. It makes the process easier, more efficient, and a lot more fun.

For Sale by Owners (FSBOs)

FSBO's are homes being marketed without the help of an agent; they are not always listed on the MLS, but your agent can still help you purchase a home that is for sale by owner. A home is for sale by owner for one of these reasons:

- The homeowner hates Realtors.
- They think they can do a lot of what a seller's agent does on their own, without paying a six percent commission.
- The homeowner does not have enough equity in the home to pay Realtor fees so they have no choice but to sell it themselves.

FSBOs have more options then ever when it comes to selling their homes. In the past, in order to get their home listed on the MLS, homeowners had no choice but to hire a Realtor to represent them and pay a six percent commission. These days, they can pay $300-$500 and have their home listed on the MLS. Once listed, every Realtor in that area can view the listing and show the home to prospective buyers. The seller offers a commission to the Realtor that brings the buyer, and they pay about half of what they normally would in commissions. This is a very smart way to sell a home, in my opinion, as long as they make it easy for Realtors to show the house.

Secret: Realtors hate working with FSBOs

Why? Homeowners typically do not know how to value their property and their homes are often priced incorrectly. I love finding a great house for sale by owner that is priced far too low, and it thrills me when my clients get a great deal. But, more often than not, the house is overpriced and working with the seller is difficult at best. I work with FSBOs all the time, but I hate it. Most will not use a lockbox, making it necessary for the seller to provide access to the property. That means I have to make an appointment with the seller directly, versus one call to a service that makes all my appointments for me, and then coordinate that time with the buyer. When I call the owner to schedule an appointment, they are always suspicious of me and generally grumpy because so many listing agents have contacted them trying to list their home. The seller insists on showing us around the house and it is awkward, since most buyers do not feel comfortable opening doors and looking in closets when the seller is present. The showing takes three times longer than usual because the seller wants to make small talk and woo the buyers. In addition, the homes are seldom worth considering because they did not have a Realtor advising them on the best way to present their home to buyers. Yes, I hate working with FSBOs.

Still, I always look for FSBOs for my clients, but not right away. Once I have a really good idea of what my buyers are looking for and where, I preview by owner homes and only take my clients to see the strong possibilities. I also do a quick Comparative Market Analysis (CMA) to see how the home is priced, and I try to get as much information about the seller and the house as possible in case my client decides to make an offer. The seller needs to have an idea of how real estate is sold in my state because I'm not their representative, and it is not my job to help the homeowner sell the house. I will not let my buyers spend a dime until I am convinced that the seller will actually close the deal. After all, the seller has nothing to lose. My buyer pays for inspections and appraisals, and they will lose hundreds of dollars if the seller does not close. It is my job to ensure that does not happen. So if your Realtor is not showing you FSBOs, do not assume it's because they are lazy or that they are trying to hide something from you. Sometimes that are protecting you from a seller who has no idea what they are doing.

New Construction

There are some advantages to buying a brand new home. First, there is the "new house smell," and the fact that no one else's feet have ever been on your carpet. More importantly, new homes offer energy saving features unmatched by homes even a few years old. A new home generally has a ten-year structural warranty, which include foundation and load bearing items, a two-year systems warranty, including electrical, plumbing, and air conditioning, and a one-year floor to ceiling warranty. However, for every positive there is a negative and, of course, the negatives range from superficial to deal killer.

You generally pay a premium for new construction, and it can take about five years before you really start to build any equity in your home. Builders start new communities where there is open land, and that generally means that your commute is going to be longer, and that you will be farther away from the center of the city. When the neighborhood is new, you really won't know what type of neighbors you will have until after you move in. The biggest risk, however, involves the condition of the house. It may take a year or more before you notice defects in the property. In my area, the risk is caused by our clay-based soil, which leads to a large number of foundation problems. In your area, it may be something different, but the assumption that homes are free of problems simply because they are new is wrong, wrong, wrong.

Types of new homes

There are three different types of new construction homes: custom homes, spec homes, and tract homes.

Custom Homes

When building a custom home, you make all the choices. You pick the lot, the builder, the architect, faucets, roof, air conditioning, and everything in between.

On the plus side, you get almost exactly what you want, and you have some control of the price, at least in theory. You move into a home that does not look like every home on the block, and you can take pride in the fact that you conceptualized your vision and saw it through to fruition.

Now - the down side. The first obstacle is finding a builder that can deliver everything he or she promises. You have to worry about the builder going over budget, running off with your money or going bankrupt, whether or not he or she can find quality labor to construct your home, and whether or not your marriage will survive the process. Chances are they will not finish on time, and in the end you will probably only get 95 percent of what you wanted. Theoretically, you could use a Realtor as a second set of eyes and ears, but you probably will not find one dumb enough to get involved.

Tract Homes

Developers who buy a large piece of land and divide it up into much smaller lots build what are known as "tract" homes and create subdivisions. When you think tract home, you might think David Weekley, Meritage Homes, Ryland Homes, First Texas, and others. Generally, the builder has 15-20 floor plans that they build in a subdivision, and they are all similar, but not identical. You pick one of the floor plans, choose your cosmetic items, customize the floor plan (depending on the builder), and six months later you have a house. Because of the volume of homes being built, and the lower costs of materials and labor, tract homes are generally far less expensive than custom homes. The price and availability are the most appealing things about tract homes. However, you should know that the quality varies not only by builder, but also by area. Do not assume that David Weekley, for example, builds the same quality product in all parts of town. The price point and their desired profit margin most certainly dictate the quality of the materials that they use, and in some areas the quality is horrific.

Spec Homes

A spec home (speculative home for sale) is simply a tract home that is being built without anyone particular in mind. Builders like to have a few homes ready, or almost ready, for buyers who need to move quickly. Sometimes a spec home is available because the original buyer backed out of the transaction for some reason. The same pros and cons that exist for tract homes are true for spec homes.

Buying a Tract or Spec Home

Buying a new tract or spec home is much different than buying a resale home, and you will find your Realtor to be an invaluable asset throughout the process, for the reasons discussed here.

Most builders use their own contract rather than the contract promulgated by the real estate commission in your area, and the contract was not written to be fair. It was written to benefit the builder, not you. And, although it varies by area, most of the salespeople at a builder's model are not Realtors; they work for the builder and are not licensed or regulated by the state. That means that they do not have a legal requirement to treat you fairly, and the only knowledge they have about construction and real estate is what they learn in their training classes. Some builder representatives are better than others, of course. There are some who know a great deal about construction, and others that know much about interior design. The one thing they all have in common, however, is that they want you to buy a house. They really don't care if you like the house, as long as you close and don't say mean things about them.

Builders welcome, and usually prefer, buyers who are represented by Realtors. Does it cost you more to use a Realtor? Sometimes. Most builders say that Realtor commissions come out of their marketing budget so the buyer is not really paying commissions, and I am sure this is true much, but not all, of the time. Generally when builders are selling spec homes, they ask the potential buyer if they have a realtor before they quote them their best price, and the price *is* higher if there is a realtor involved. But you should not begrudge a Realtor the fee they are paid for their expertise; they are there to keep you from getting ripped off. If you did not have a Realtor, you would have to pay a lawyer, and lawyers don't know very much about buying a home, beyond the contracts and title work. If you plan to have your Realtor represent you in the purchase a spec home or to help you build a tract home, be sure you mention to the sales person that you have representation on your *first visit*. Or, better yet, give the builder your Realtor's card and tell him to contact them, instead of you, with information. It will send a signal that they are not going to be able to rip you off, and it will guarantee that the builder works with your Realtor, since some builders require that your agent be with you on your first visit to their model.

What You Need to Know About New Construction

Spec homes are often listed on the MLS, so your Realtor can show them to you just like any other MLS listed home. If you visit the model on your own, the onsite salesperson can show you a list of their homes that are available immediately or within a month or two. Here are some things you should know about buying a spec or building a tract home.

Builders are most anxious to sell their spec homes first, and here is why. The interest rate for homes under construction (construction financing) is far lower than homes that are finished and move-in ready. It is expensive for builders to keep homes in inventory, so spec homes are generally far more negotiable than build jobs, especially if you can close quickly.

- Builders do not like to reduce their prices and risk upsetting other buyers who pay more. You can generally expect a small reduction in price but a large number of "free" upgrades like tile or granite.

- The home you buy will look *nothing* like the model. Builders use higher quality materials in their models, and their models are staged to attract buyers. In fact, there is an entire industry dedicated to the cause. I suggest you do not even walk through the model, unless you are just looking for decorating ideas. Look at one of their spec homes or a build job that is near completion. Do not be fooled by their smoke and mirrors.

- You still need an inspection on a new home. In fact, you need it more since you will be the first person to live in the house.

- If you are building a home, the salesperson will want to write the contract to reflect a sales price plus a detailed list of upgrades, and you are expected to decide what you want before you even go to the design center. A better way is to negotiate a dollar amount or a budget to use at the design center.

- When building, be sure to insist on an inspection before the sheetrock goes up to ensure that the space between the studs is clean. It is not uncommon for workers to leave trash and food in the empty house and for garbage and sawdust to be left in between the walls.

- Do not ever, ever, ever buy a home from a builder before researching their reputation online. And do not be afraid to talk to neighbors and find out about their experiences.

- Although new homes come with all kinds of warranties, do not assume the builder is going to honor them, even when they use a third-party warranty company. Warranty companies go out of business all the time, and they have all kinds of "out" clauses that they can use to get out of fixing your house. It is best to pretend that you are buying a resale home, and hope you get lucky when you file a warranty claim.

- Builders have preferred lenders, or may even own their own mortgage companies and title companies. They will often offer you $5,000 in closing costs, for example, if you use their lender. They will claim that their rates are competitive, but you *must* shop around and do your due diligence. Builders will say they prefer their own lenders because they can control the loan process, but that is not true. Owning a mortgage company is another profit center for the builders. As a buyer, it's all about the math. The cheapest loan, after factoring in the builder's contribution to your closing costs, gets your business. Cost means total cost, not upfront cost. You are losing money if the builder gives you $5,000 in closing costs but offers you a 4.5 percent interest rate, when you can get 4.25 percent or less through another mortgage company; in the long run, you will save *a lot* more than $5,000 when you get a loan with lower interest rate. Do not be held hostage by $5,000, and the games builders play. Most of my buyers find it is cheaper to use their own lenders.

- Builders also offer incentives to use their title company, if they are affiliated with one. The incentive is that they will pay for your title policy. If the title incentive is separate from the mortgage incentive, it can be a pretty good deal. If not, it is, once again, all about the math.

I understand the allure of buying a brand new home. Have a good agent represent you but do your research, do the math, and hope for the best.

Foreclosures and Short Sales

When a homeowner stops making his or her mortgage payment, the bank takes back the house in a process called foreclosure. A short sale is a house that sells for less than the balance on its mortgage. Banks must approve short sales and it is typically in their best interest to do so since they will recoup more money than they would if the house went into foreclosure.

The techniques to buy property that has been foreclosed upon, and the risks involved in doing so are beyond the scope of this book. My experience with foreclosures has demonstrated to me that it is difficult to make the math work. Let's say there is a bank owned property (foreclosure) that interests you, and that the sales price is$200,000 and you estimate that the home needs roughly $35,000worth of repairs and improvements. Your Realtor analyzes the market for you and determines that homes of similar size in good condition sell for an average of $245,000. Assuming you do not have any unexpected surprises, you fix up the house and make a $10,000 profit. Is $10,000 enough to justify the substantial risk and effort involved with buying properties that are typically in poor condition? To some, it is. It was to me when I first started flipping homes. I soon realized I was making below minimum wage for my efforts, and learned that I had to start buying homes cheaper if I was going to make a living as a flipper.

It is very difficult, in my opinion, to buy a foreclosed upon house cheap enough to make it worth the trouble and to justify the risk. The only exception I have found involves very high-end luxury homes costing over a million dollars. So, if you are in the market for a multi-million dollar home, you should keep your eyes open for a good foreclosure. Otherwise - buyer beware.

Short sales can be worth pursuing under certain circumstances. The problem, however, is that the bank can takes several weeks, or even months, to approve the contract. If you are looking at short sales, focus on the ones that already have bank approval, and save yourself weeks of not knowing if you are going to be able to buy a particular house. It's just not smart to tie your money up that way.

Buying a home without a Realtor

If you have found a home or have a relationship with someone selling his or her home, you can hire a Realtor or real estate consultant to manage the transaction for you. The Realtor would be a neutral third-party participant to the transaction who would write the offers and amendments, manage inspections, and guide both the seller and buyer through the closing. The cost is generally split between the buyer and the seller. You may have to find an independent agent since many of the larger real estate brokerages will not work this way.

CHAPTER THREE
House Hunting

Get the Dogs Out

Go through the list you received from your Realtor and get rid of the "dogs." Dogs are homes that have structural problems, are bordered by power lines or commercial property, or are obviously dumps, unless you are looking for a fixer upper, of course. You can generally eliminate many homes just by looking at the pictures and reading the description. If you received an electronic list, you will be able to view many pictures of each home, and even take virtual tours.

If you want a home in pristine condition, get rid of anything that says, "handyman special" or "bring your decorating ideas." If you want to rehab a home, get rid of homes that say, "Mrs. Clean lives here," or "Pristine!" Do not eliminate too many homes based strictly on the exterior because the interior may be spectacular and worth a look. Landscaping is easy to fix. Your goal is to get rid of the homes that obviously will not work for you. The ones that make the first cut are now "Possibilities."

Narrowing Down the Possibilities

Possibilities are homes worth further exploration. Start narrowing down your Possibilities list by going to Google Maps to see what surrounds the house. If you notice that the back of the property is bordered by power lines, commercial property, busy streets, or railroad tracks, move it to the 'Reject' pile.

As you go through your list, you'll find homes that really excite you, and others about which you are uncertain. Move the ones that excite you to your "Favorites" pile and leave the rest in "Possibilities." Send both lists to your agent, and schedule some time to visit your Favorites. Once your agent has a good idea what you like, he or she can explore your "Possibilities" list for you and take you to see ones that might work. Your agent will learn a lot about you based on the homes you chose.

Viewing Homes

On your first visit to a home, see if you like the way it feels before you spend too much time there. If the condition of the home activates your gag reflex, move on. You will be surprised by how many homes that look beautiful from the outside are actually dogs on the inside. You will not hurt your agent's feelings if you don't like the house, and there is no point in wasting time in a house that you hate. If you find that you like the way the house feels, analyze the floor plan and try to envision how you would live there. As you are walking through, make mental notes about the general condition of the house. Keep your eyes open for cracks in the walls, slanted floors, water damage, mold, and other troublesome areas. Listed here are some other things to consider when viewing a house.

Floor Plans

The flow of the house needs to make sense. You need the right number of rooms and a place for everyone in the family to work, play and sleep. Because people live differently, floor plans are not "one size fits all." Here are some general rules that apply to most people:

Formal Living & Dining – Combo

I usually try to steer buyers away from the "combo" or stacked plan (see Figure 1). In a combo plan, the formal living room and formal dining room are one large space, which takes up much of the front of the house. Most people do not want formal lives spaces anymore, favoring home office space instead. In a combo plan, there is a lot of wasted space. Look for split formals rather than stacked formals, discussed next.

Figure 1: Living Room/Dining Room - Combo

Formal Living & Dining – Split

A split formal floor plan has the dining room on one side of the front door and the formal living room on the other. Adding French doors to the formal living room will transform it into a home office.

Figure 2: Split Formals

Open Concept Kitchen/Family Room

An open concept kitchen is one in which the kitchen, breakfast room, and family room exist as one large space rather than smaller sectioned areas. Generally speaking, this types of space is very, very popular.

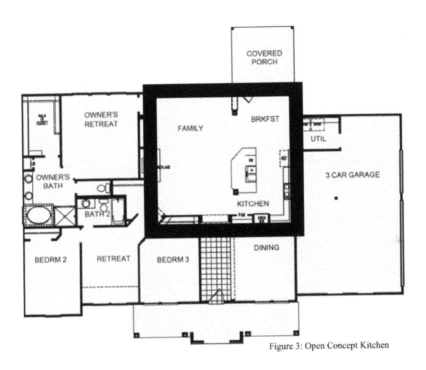

Figure 3: Open Concept Kitchen

Master Bedroom

A large percentage of newer homes have the master bedroom on the first floor. The perceived benefit is that the adults are downstairs and the kids are upstairs, so the downstairs area stays neater and quieter. Some buyers have learned the hard way that it is extremely inconvenient to have a new baby in a nursery on the second floor, away from Mom and Dad. The choice is yours. Today's buyers still favor a downstairs master, even knowing that the crib and changing table may end up in a corner in the master bedroom, at least for a while.

Be mindful of the location of the downstairs master bedroom. The location preferred by most is in the back of the house, but there should be at least a small hallway to separate the master bedroom from the family room. In other words, you should not be able to look into the master bedroom from the family room.

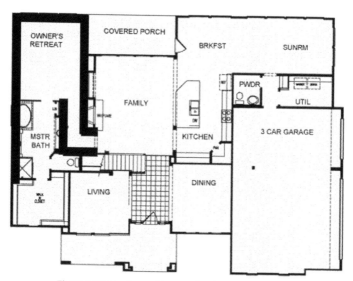

Figure 4: Master down with separation from family room

Master bedrooms located in the front of the house are not nearly as desirable as ones located in the back. Though not necessarily a deal killer, you will lose buyers when it is time to resell the home. An ideal and highly sought after floor plan is one with both the master and a second bedroom downstairs, and two or three bedrooms upstairs, as pictured next.

Figure 5: Master Front & Second Bedroom Down

Kitchen

An ideal floor plan is one in which the garage opens into the utility room, which leads to the kitchen, so you do not have to carry your groceries from the garage across the house to the kitchen. See the following example. Also illustrated in this example is the odd location of the utility room, next to the formal living spaces.

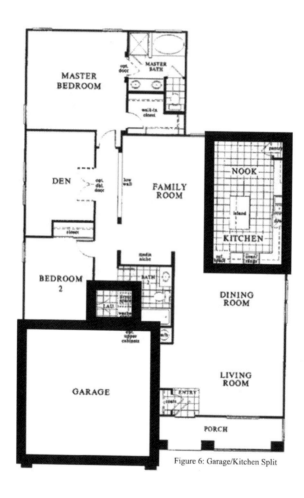

Figure 6: Garage/Kitchen Split

Split Bedrooms

In single story homes, homes with a three-way split allow family members some privacy. As can be see in Figure 7, below, bedrooms are located on opposite sides of the home, separated by the family room.

Figure 7: Split Bedrooms

Resale

The secret to buying a home with good resale potential is to buy one that will attract the largest pool of buyers. Stated differently, don't buy a home that has a feature that no one in their right mind would want! That means none of the following: homes in bad locations next to busy streets, schools, commercial property, power lines, etc., homes without a garage, pantry, or linen closet, homes that have the smallest yard in the neighborhood, homes with small closets, etc. The owners of these type of homes will try to distract you with beautiful landscaping, hardwood floors, and stainless steel appliances. Don't be the buyer of someone else's problem. Just don't do it!

Property Condition

If you are working with an exclusive buyer agent, he or she will undoubtedly be able to help you spot obvious flaws in the condition of the home, and will recognize unpopular floor plans. Realtors are not inspectors, but you should be able to rely on them to point out obvious issues like roof and foundation problems. My personal guarantee to my buyer/clients is that if the inspection uncovers something that leads them to walk away from the house, I will pay for their next inspection.

The seller is required to disclose everything to you that he knows to be wrong with the property. Between your agent and the seller, you should have a pretty good idea of the condition of the property before you hire an inspector. The following includes some general guidelines on what to look for when evaluating a property. Note that different materials are used in different parts of the country, and this list is not meant to be all- inclusive.

Roof

If the roof is more than 15-20 years old, chances are it needs to be replaced. But younger roofs can also fail. Look for shingles that are lifting up, cracked or missing, with curled edges, and take note of areas where the granules have worn off. Also look for water stains on the underside of the roof and on the ceiling.

Foundation

Foundation problems are usually caused by bad drainage, ground movement, or poor construction, which causes the foundation to shift or settle. Signs of foundation problems include doors and windows that no longer open or close, drywall cracks and cracks in the bricks. Less obvious clues are cracks in the slab that can sometimes be seen on vinyl floors, cracked tiles that do not lay flat, and a slanted floor.

Sprinkler

It is very common for sprinkler heads to break, usually when someone runs over them with the lawn mower. The control box located in the garage turns the system on and off, and is usually zoned for front, back and sides. Be certain you know what you are buying. Some homes only have sprinklers installed in the front or back. You do not want to overpay for the home because you have assumed the yard is fully sprinklered.

Air Conditioners and Heaters

Your inspector will test the heater and air conditioner to verify their operability, but it is important that you get an idea of their age and general condition before you make an offer. Take a look at both the inside and outside units, and take note of dust and rust in the vents. Improper maintenance will significantly shorten the life of heating and cooling systems. If the units are very old or seem to be neglected, be sure to factor the replacement cost into your offer.

Windows

When air gets between the two pieces of glass in a double pane window, the condensation can cause foggy windows. The only fix for this is to replace the glass. Your inspector will check each and every window, but try to get a general idea of their condition before you make an offer. If the house needs all new windows, the cost will run into the thousands.

Plumbing

Your inspector will check the plumping system, but take note of leaking faucets, showerheads, and toilets, and also ascertain the age of the water heater by looking at the label on the unit. If the water heater is old and located in the attic, you will want it replaced since a leak will damage the inside of the house. If it is located in the garage, gas water heaters must be on a stand eighteen inches off the floor and they must have an expansion tank. Straps are required in earthquake zones.

Exposer

The direction a house faces is called its "exposer," and is a matter of personal preference. In some cultures, an east facing home is considered lucky and the buyer will not consider any other exposer. If the front of a house faces north, the back yard has more sun in the summer. Homes facing south generally have shade in the backyard in the afternoon, which is desirable in warmer climates. The floor plan and location of the rooms will determine the comfort level of the home.

Pests

Your lender may require a certificate from your inspector stating that the home is free of termites and other critters. Even if it is not a lender requirement, you will definitely want to know if the home has an active termite infestation or has been treated in the past. If prior treatments to the property have occurred, find out if they were partial treatments or if the whole house was treated. Sometimes if only one side of the house is treated, the termites will simply move from one side of the house to the other.

Lead Based Paint

Homes built before 1978 may have been painted with lead based paint. The seller or their agent is required to give you the EPA booklet called "Protect Your Family From Lead in Your Home".

The seller must disclose any known lead-based paint hazards, and give you any relevant records. The risk with lead based paint is when children or pets ingest it, since the lead can cause brain damage. Typically homes that originally had lead based paint have been re-painted many times through the years, and this reduces the risks substantially.

Environmental Hazards

Sellers are also required to disclose any known environmental hazards like leaking underground oil tanks, the presence of radon or asbestos, and lead pipes, among others. There can be serious health and financial consequences associated with the clean up of these hazards; know what you are buying and what risks you are assuming.

Floodplains

You need to know if the home is located in a floodplain. If it is, your lender is going to require flood insurance. The extra expense may or may not be a deal breaker, but you are entitled to know your risks and responsibilities before you sign on the dotted line. You can go to http://www.floodsmart.gov/floodsmart/ to review the flood maps in your area.

Nuisance Factors

When you are at the house, listen for things that can make you crazy, like barking dogs, traffic from local schools or restaurants, airplanes, trains, and noise from distant freeways. Remember, even if it doesn't bother you during the day, the noise may make you nuts at night.

Narrowing It Down

The truth is that the perfect house does not exist. Even people who build a custom home find things they wish they had designed differently. With any luck, you will find yourself with a short list of two or three homes. So, how do you decide which home to buy? The secret to buying a home without losing your shirt is to first use your head, then use your heart.

As they did in the old days, get out your yellow legal pad. First, draw a line down the middle of the page and write the positive aspects of your prospective house on one side and the negative aspects on the other side; each finalist gets their own page. Hopefully, you have already eliminated homes in bad locations, with bad foundations, and unlivable floor plans, and you are left with homes that are perfectly safe investments with good potential for resale. Rank your choices, and compare and contrast the top two.

The Top Two

You still need more information about your top choices. Ask your agent to send you the following documents on each home:

Comparable Marketing Analysis (CMA)

Your agent will research information about comparable properties in the area using the MLS, including active listings, pending sales, and expired listings. After making adjustments for property condition and other factors, he or she will recommend a sales price for the home. Do not be surprised if a price range is recommended, rather than a firm price. By reviewing the CMA, you will know immediately if the house is priced too high or too low.

NOTE: It is very easy for your Realtor to manipulate the numbers to make it appear that a home is worth more or less than is actually the case. Ask your agent to send you all the raw data that they used in their report, including active listings, expired listings, sold listings, and listings that are sold but haven't closed yet. Hopefully they don't "accidently on purpose" forgot to send you a listing that would have a major impact on the pricing of the home.

Price/Square Foot

Larger homes are priced lower per square foot, and smaller homes are priced higher per square foot. Why? The value of the land has to be concentrated into the price of the home. The smaller the home, the more the value is concentrated.

It is not helpful to take an average of the price per square foot of homes in the neighborhood and multiply it by the square footage to come up with an offer. However, the information is useful in tracking trends and ensuring that the home is priced comparably to other homes of the same size and condition.

Seller's Disclosure Report

It might be called something different in your state, but sellers are required by law to disclose everything that they know about the property. In Texas, they do so on a form promulgated by the Texas Real Estate Commission, called the Seller's Disclosure Report. From this report you will learn the age and condition of all of the components in the house.

Review this report very carefully and remember that the accuracy of these reports is contingent upon the seller's knowledge of the property and his or her integrity. Yes, some sellers lie in order to present their home in the best possible light. That is why you need an inspector.

Tax Rolls

You or your agent can go online to the county tax assessor's website and uncover all types of information about the property. While you are investigating, try to uncover the following:

Discrepancies in Square Footage

The square footage listed in the tax rolls can be substantially different than the square footage the seller claims. A 100 square foot variance at $90/square foot is $9,000! Know what you're buying.

Tax Assessed Value (TAV)

The TAV is not the same thing as market value; do not assume for a second that the TAV is the price you should pay for the house. You pay property taxes based on the TAV, and this figure is typically lower than market value. If this figure is higher than what your agent told you the house was worth, investigate why this may be the case. Also look to see if the TAV has been increased or decreased each year. If it is consistently on a downward trend, then you may be in an area with depreciating values. Why are prices dropping? It could be that the area was overvalued in the first place, but you need to know for sure. Or, it could just be indicative of the real estate market in general.

Neighborhood Demographics and Factoids

Most agents have access to this type of information and can present it to you in a pretty little package. You do not have to guess who your neighbors are; the information is out there for free! Use this information like pieces of a puzzle to learn everything you can about the property and area *before* you write an offer and spend any money.

History Report

It's not hard to learn the history of the property. On the tax assessor's website, you should be able to learn when the seller purchased the house and from whom, and how many other previous owners there were. You can often find out how much the seller paid and the amount of his or her original loan. It helps to know how much equity a homeowner has, if you can figure it out. If, for example, seller owes more than what the house is worth at today's prices, the seller is "upside down" and will need to take money to the closing table. You need to make sure that they have the cash to sell the house. If not, you're dealing with a short sale transaction, which was discussed earlier.

CHAPTER FOUR
Offers and Negotiations

Making an Offer

This is when the gamesmanship starts, and this is why you need a strong negotiator to represent you. Before you make an offer, have your agent call the seller's agent to see if they have any offers or contracts. You do not want to lose your second choice home if your first choice is sold. This call is an opportunity for your agent to learn why the seller is moving and how desperate he or she is to sell the home. If the listing agent is practically begging for an offer, you can submit a lower offer.

The seller might be in the midst of negotiating a contract with another buyer. If they have verbalized a deal and is just waiting for signatures, it is time to move on. Or, if you really love the house, you can still submit an offer and the seller's agent will be required to present it to the seller/client. If nothing else, your contract can be in a backup position.

The seller's agent will undoubtedly tell your agent to submit your best offer to try to knock out the first buyer. In very competitive markets, you really may have to submit your best price, but in my area I typically advise my clients not to play that game. I prefer to submit roughly the same offer I would otherwise, but really sell my client's credentials and commitment to close. I also encourage my buyers to accommodate the seller's closing time frame, if at all possible. Your first goal should be beat out the other buyer, and next to negotiate the price and terms. Being flexible in your closing date can help you accomplish this.

Sometimes the seller's agent will state that they are expecting an offer on the property "any minute" and will encourage you to submit an offer ASAP. Or, he or she will tell you how many people have expressed an interest in the house and will try to convince you that the home is going to sell very quickly. These are obvious sales tactics used to generate an offer on the property.

Your agent cannot know for sure if the other agent is being truthful or if they are just playing games. Take a look at how long the home has been on the market. If it is a new listing and it is a great house, the agent might be telling the truth. If it has been on the market for over a month or two, there probably is no bidding war, and the agent is probably playing games.

Initial Offer

Based on everything you have learned while researching the property, you need to come up with your initial offer. This amount will be based on the property condition, days on market, the CMA that your agent produced, and what you perceive as the seller's determination to sell the home. I use the word 'perceived' because you never really know what the seller's situation is. Price is not the only negotiable item to include when you write an offer. If you know that you are going to ask for a carpet allowance, include that in your initial offer. If you know of certain repairs that you require, ask for them up front. You can be specific about the closing date, or leave it blank and let the seller choose the date. Your agent will generate the paperwork for you and write the offer based on the laws in your state. After getting your signatures and any required deposits, they will present the offer to the seller's agent, who will then present it to the seller.

Competing Offers

If you believe that there truly is a competing buyer for a house that you want, have your agent call the seller's agent and let him know you are writing an offer, and tell him to see what they can learn about the seller's situation. Are they relocating? Have they found another place to live? How quickly do they need to move?

Do not assume that you need to pay more to beat out the other guy. If you can be flexible with your closing date, it is often more important to the seller than the cash. It is extremely stressful to sell a house. If you can accommodate the seller's needs it will go a long way in helping you win the offer war.

Negotiating Strategies

After your offer is presented to the seller, he or she has the option to accept your offer, reject your offer, or make a counter-offer. Remember that everything is negotiable, not just the price. In my eighteen years in the industry, I have noticed a few patterns in the way sellers respond to the offers I submit on behalf of my buyer/clients. They include:

The Cave

The Seller accepts the offer with no changes. They agree to the price, closing date, home warranty, title policy, closing costs, etc. This only happens with the most desperate sellers, typically ones who are in danger of losing the home. On deals like these, the seller usually has little or no money to make repairs, so be prepared to buy the house "as is".

Seller comes down in price by $1000

This means that they think your initial offer is ridiculous but they do want to try to work with you. It is an invitation for you to submit a better offer. This type of response upsets some buyers, which I do not understand. The initial offer gives a lot of information about the seller's circumstances and level of motivation: it means they are not desperate and are not going to give the house away.

Baby Steps

Here, the seller responds to your offer by dropping $3,000-$4,000. As a buyer, you respond by coming up $3,000-$4000, and so forth. The parties go back and forth until one or the other claims it is his or her final offer, usually after the third round.

Split the difference

Some sellers hate to negotiate, and view it as confrontational. These people just want to split the difference and get it over with. I've found that's it is usually quite easy to get the seller to reduce their asking price a little more in this scenario, if not with price than with other negotiable items like repairs.

What Not to Do

Some buyers are their own worst enemies. Here are some things buyers do during negotiations that cost them money.

They have a long list of complaints about house.

Some unsophisticated buyers like to present the seller with a long list of things that they think are wrong with the house in order to get a better price. This "I'm doing you a favor by buying your home" attitude does nothing but antagonize the seller, and creates an unfriendly and risky transaction. If the buyer is making an offer to purchase a property, he or she clearly likes the house and sees value in owning it. If the seller has an opportunity to sell the home to someone more pleasant, they will. And if they don't, they are not going to care for and leave the house in good condition when they leave. Play nice or pay a price.

They use their hearts, not their heads.

The homebuying process is tedious, stressful and, at times, exhausting. There are few decisions greater than this one! By the time you pick a house you are going to be emotionally invested. This is where you really need a good agent to be your voice of reason. Control your emotions until after repairs have been negotiated, and you are sure it is a good house.

They overpay because they are afraid of losing the house.

There are definitely times when you have to submit your best offer, but more often than not there is plenty of room for negotiation. Take an objective look at the seller's situation, the general real estate climate in your area, and at the data that your agent provides, to see how long it takes similar homes to sell in your area. If the home has a unique feature that can't be found anywhere else, you may need to pay more. If you can find a home similar to this one on any given block, don't submit your best offer right away.

Counter Offers & Acceptance

Once you make your initial offer, the seller will respond as described above. You will know immediately which strategy the seller is using and you will know how to respond. I strongly recommend that you keep asking for discounts until the seller says "no" twice. If, for example, you have gone three rounds with the seller and they come back with their best and final offer, don't believe them. Make another counter offer and see what happens. If they still say no, go ahead and accept.

Contingencies

A contingency in your contract will allow you to back out of the deal without penalty if anything goes wrong. Some Realtors will say that buyers use them because they are not sure that they want to buy the house. These Realtors work for the seller. As a buyer, you do not want to spend money inspecting and appraising a home if the seller is not legally obligated to sell you the home once you do. Writing a contract with contingencies allows you the time you need to do your due diligence. Here are some common contract contingencies:

Financing contingency

A financing contingency says that your offer is contingent upon you being able to secure financing for the property within a certain period of time. It specifies in detail the type of financing, the terms, and how long you have to obtain loan approval. Unless you are buying a home with cash, you should always include a Financing Contingency. If your financing falls through, at least you'll get your deposit back. Generally, twenty days is plenty of time for you to secure financing. The deal does not have to close in twenty days, but you should have your loan approved with "conditions." Conditional loan approval means that the bank will lend you money once certain conditions are met, like the appraisal, job verification, a certain bank statement, and so forth.

Appraisal Contingency

The appraisal contingency has become an important one in some parts of the country where home prices have dropped significantly. The appraisal contingency says that if the house does not appraise for at least the purchase price, you can back out of the deal. You can also write it to say that if the house doesn't appraise for the purchase price, the seller has to drop the price; if he or she refuses to do so, you can back of the deal without penalty. Truth be told, if the house does not appraise, the bank will not lend you the money you need to buy the house. You will either have to pay cash for the difference (don't do this!), the seller will have to drop the price, or you have to walk away from the deal.

Inspection Contingency or Option Period

Some states call this an "Option Period," and others call it a "Due Diligence Contingency." This contingency allows the buyer a certain period of time (I recommend 7-10 days) to get the home inspected, along with anything else they need to do to be certain that they want to buy the property. The buyer can back out of the deal for any reason at all without penalty, and he or she can use this period of time to renegotiate repairs with the seller after the inspection. Some states require that the buyer pay an "option fee" to the seller. Option fees are discussed later in this chapter.

Contingency for Sale of Another Property

This contingency is for buyers who have to sell their current homes before they can buy a new one. Basically, it allows the buyer the right to back out of the deal if he or she cannot sell their current home. Contracts can also be written with a "kick-out" clause, which allows the seller to "kick out" the original contract if they find a new buyer that can close right away.

Option Fee & Earnest Money

An option fee is money paid by a buyer to a seller for the option to terminate the real estate contract. An option gives the buyer time to have the house inspected and negotiate repairs, while at the same time it restricts the seller from selling the house to someone else. Buyers can terminate the contract during the option period for any reason. I write my contracts so that the buyer loses their option fee if they terminate the contract, but they get the money back if they close the transaction. The amount of the option fee is generally between $50 and $250 in my area. Note that not all states use options when buying and selling property, although everything is negotiable.

Option fee funds should not be confused with earnest money. Earnest money is a security deposit that demonstrates the buyer's commitment to purchasing the property, and is a show of good faith. The amount of earnest money is negotiable. Generally, you want to keep the amount of earnest money to a minimum, but high enough that the seller takes your offer seriously. Earnest money is placed in a trust account, and in some states, it is held by the title company. In other states the seller's broker may hold it. Earnest money is applied to the buyer's down payment and closing costs. If there is a failure to close through no fault of the buyer, the seller usually signs an agreement to release the funds back to the buyer, and vice-versa, if the seller fails to close. Disputes do arise, however, and that is when you really need to be able to rely on your agent to get your money back.

CHAPTER FIVE
Inspections & Property Condition

Hiring an inspector

You definitely need to hire a professional inspector to go through every square inch of the house and report the findings. Your inspector should be experienced and come recommended from a friend, co-worker, or your Realtor. Be aware, however, of potential conflicts of interest if you rely on a recommendation from your Realtor. Hopefully, your Realtor will give you a list of inspectors to choose from and you can make your own choice.

Personally, I recommend inspectors based on the quality of their reports, but I do not have personal relationships with them, nor have I even met most of them. I do not attend inspections in order to give my clients the opportunity to discuss the condition of the house with a neutral party to the transaction. If I have a question about an item on the report, I email the inspector and always include my client in the communication. The inspectors work for my clients, not for me, and I welcome their advice and expertise.

A good inspection should take about three to four hours, depending on the size of the house, and in the end you will have a list of items that are in need of repair or replacement, and you will have learned how to maintain the property. Your inspector should go through each item with you. Be certain you understand the report so that you can make good choices when requesting repairs from the seller.

Which Repairs to Request

Even when you are buying new construction, you do not get a perfect house. Do not expect the seller to agree to all the repairs. Once you submit your repair request, negotiations are on again. Here are some guidelines:

Roof

Find out the condition of the roof and try to estimate the remaining life. If there is existing damage from hail, for example, be sure that the seller files a claim with their insurance company, and do not close until the roof is either replaced or the money is held in escrow (the title company holds the money and pays the roofer once the repair has been made). This is non-negotiable since you may have a problem getting homeowner's insurance on the property if there is existing damage. Do not incur any additional expenses until this issue is resolved! If you need to walk away from the house, you want to lose as little money as possible.

Sprinkler

With the exception of broken sprinkler heads, I do not like my clients to assume the risk of a broken sprinkler system. Repairs can be expensive and leaks hard to locate. Have the seller make any repairs before closing.

Appliances

Typically, only built-in appliances are included in the sale of a home, at least that is the case in Texas. Ovens, ranges, built-in microwaves, and dishwashers are relatively low cost items to repair/replace. If these items are working when you close on the house, they will be covered by any home warranty that you have in place.

Foundation

With very few exceptions, I advise my clients to walk away from homes that have existing or previous foundation repairs. One of the riskiest things you can do is to buy a home that needs a foundation repair. The house can be damaged during a repair (particularly the plumbing), and you cannot be certain that the repair will hold. In addition, you must disclose the repair to potential buyers of your home and the home will sell for less. In addition, you can't trust the foundation repair company to honor their warranty, or to be in business as long as you own the house. Leave foundation issues to the investors.

Air Conditioners and Heaters

Both air conditioning and heating units can be extremely costly to repair or replace, and you should insist that the seller make any necessary repairs before closing. It is especially important to clean the a/c coils if they are found to be dirty. Coils become dirty when the homeowner fails to change the filters on a regular basis. Because this is considered to be a maintenance item, cleaning the coils is typically excluded from your home warranty, and is an expensive fix that you shouldn't have to incur.

Windows

One of the most common issues I see pertains to double pane windows. When air gets between the two panes of glass in a double pane window, it can lead to condensation and fog. The only fix is to replace the glass. I typically advise my clients to request the repair of foggy windows when they are in highly visible locations. If the majority of the windows are faulty, I recommend replacement of all the windows, or cash in lieu of replacement since the cost to replace all of the windows will be several thousand dollars.

Cosmetics

Paint, faucets, flooring, and sealant/trim are what I consider to be cosmetic items. I always recommend that my clients take care of these items themselves after the sale. The seller usually tries to save money by making the repairs themselves and the results are usually not good. If the home is in need of substantial cosmetic updating, you need to pay less for the house or get a decorating allowance.

Plumbing

With the exception of small leaks or minor items, the seller needs to make all plumbing repairs and assume the risk. This includes repairs to the hot water heater, especially if the water heater is in the attic.

Repair Allowances

Under certain circumstances, you may wish to ask for cash in lieu of repairs, or to ask for cash in addition to certain repairs. As previously mentioned, there are repairs that are best handled by you, the buyer.

Many times sellers would prefer not to have to deal with the inconvenience of repairing the property; psychologically they have already moved on to the next house. Talk to your agent about how much it might cost to repair certain items and then see what the sellers are willing to do.

When to Walk Away

If you have done your homework in advance, and if you are working with a skilled career agent, the inspection should not reveal any big surprises. However, if something major comes up during inspection you have some decisions to make. It's reasonable to expect to buy a home with a solid roof, working electrical, plumbing, and cooling/heating systems. If any of these items need to be replaced, you should be buying the home below market value, (that is, the low end of the range on your CMA, or requesting that the seller make the repair or provide a repair allowance. These problems can be fixed. The question is who pays for it. If the issue is something major, it is time to cut your losses and move on; you certainly do not want to buy someone else's problem.

So what is considered "major?" You should walk away from anything that would prevent a future buyer from wanting to buy the house. If a future buyer wouldn't want it, you shouldn't want it either. Things like foundation problems, toxic mold, multiple termite treatments, violent deaths on the property, a basement that floods frequently, asbestos, radon, are good reasons to pass on buying the property. Air conditioners and roofs can be replaced. The stench of a double homicide in the house lives forever.

Other Points of Negotiation

There are other issues besides price that warrant tough negotiations. The following section discusses these issues.

Possession

A seller vacating the property and a buyer taking possession is the source of many potential conflicts. The sellers do not want to leave the home until they are absolutely certain that the transaction has closed, and buyers are not always comfortable with sellers living in homes that they just purchased. What if they won't leave?

The customary procedures vary based on state. In California, for example, the buyer does not take possession until the deed is actually recorded. In Texas, it's common for the seller to be given 48 hours to vacate the property after closing. If the property happens to be vacant, the buyers can usually take possession right after funding.

The terms of possession must be agreed upon before you execute your purchase offer, and the specifics must be committed to in writing! You should never, ever, ever, let the sellers stay in the home after closing without a signed Temporary Lease Agreement. If they refuse to vacate the property you will need a lease to evict them. If you do not utilize a lease agreement, you will be required to go to court for the eviction. Be sure to include in your lease a holdover fee, so if the seller does not move out on time you are compensated.

If the seller is only going to be leasing the property for 48 hours, I generally do not request a deposit or rent. It's a goodwill gesture, and I always hope that if my buyer makes it easy for the seller to move to their next home, the seller will take good care of the property and clean the house on their way out. If the seller is going to stay any longer than that, I ask the title company to hold back a few hundred dollars from the seller's proceeds in case the property is damaged. If they leave without incident, the money is promptly released.

Earnest Money

The purpose of earnest money is to show that you are sincere about purchasing the property. In a hot market, you may have to put up more earnest money to appear more interested in the house than a competing buyer. In slow markets or with desperate sellers you can get away with less. As long as you abide by the terms of the contract, you get your money back at closing as a credit against your closing costs or down payment. Your Realtor should have contingencies in your contract, as discussed earlier, to protect your earnest money in case the house does not appraise, your financing falls through, or if the house is uninsurable.

Closing Date

Accommodating the seller with respect to the closing date is an easy way to steal a house from another buyer. The seller doesn't want to move out of their house until it's sold; they don't want two housing payments. In addition, in most cases they can't buy a new home until their current home sells and closes. Anything a buyer can do to make it easier on the seller is going to mean more to the seller than cash.

If a house is vacant, the seller will be very happy with a quick closing. In my area, a quick closing is three weeks. If you can close quickly, the seller will sell for less since they won't have to make their next month's mortgage payment. If the home is still occupied, the seller may or may not have anyplace to go. Working around their schedule and making their move as easy on them as possible can save you thousands. If it turns out that you can't accommodate their needs, you're a nice guy for making the offer.

Closing Costs

When a seller pays your closing costs, the benefit for you is that it takes less cash to buy the house. You do not really save the money; the closing costs get rolled into your mortgage.

Sellers will never have a problem paying your closing costs because they are only concerned about their net. If you need help with closing costs, by all means ask for it. The following two offers are the same to the seller:

Offer One		Offer Two	
Sales Price:	$205,000	Sales Price:	$200,000
Seller paid closing costs:	$ 5,000	Seller paid closing costs:	$ 0,000
Seller's net proceeds	$200,000	Seller's net proceeds	$200,000

Lenders restrict the amount of the seller's contribution, usually to three percent. Check with your lender regarding any limits or restrictions.

CHAPTER SIX
Financing

All About Mortgages

I started talking about predatory lending and improper homebuying practices over 18 years ago. I received a lot of hate mail and even anonymous threats from mortgage 'professionals' (aka mob bosses) who did not want their secrets revealed. Today, lenders are required to be more transparent in their pricing and loan programs. Unfortunately, the policies designed to protect consumers are inadequate and the majority of loan officers are under trained order takers, rather than educated financial advisors. Due to the economic downturn, lenders are more desperate for business than ever before, and even highly educated consumers are exceedingly easy to manipulate. I spend a lot of time educating my buyers before we ever really talk seriously about buying. The following pages are intended to "give it to you in a nutshell." Education is vital if we are going to eliminate predatory lending practices. Let's get started.

Some Definitions

Mortgage brokers hire loan officers to sell loans to consumers. Mortgage brokers have accounts with wholesale lenders, who are the actual source of the funds. Each day, the wholesale lenders will provide the mortgage brokers, and all their loan officers, with wholesale rate sheets. The mortgage broker decides how much profit he or she wants to make on each loan and creates a retail rate sheet. The loan officers sell from the retail rate sheet. The difference between the wholesale rate, the retail rate *and* closing fees make up the lender's profit margin.

How Mortgage Brokers Make Money

Mortgage brokers make money several different ways. They can manipulate these potential profit avenues all day long to come up with their desired profit. The following sections describe the various ways mortgage brokers make money.

Closing costs

This includes fees for applications, credit reports, appraisals, processing, underwriting, document preparation, and so forth. These fees are sometimes referred to as "junk fees."

Origination fees

Origination fees are usually one percent of the loan amount. This is simply a fee that the broker charges for writing the loan.

Discount Points

Points are prepaid interest. They are usually only charged when the buyer wants an interest rate that is below market rates. Discount points are expressed as a percentage of the loan amount. One point is equal to one percent of the loan amount, three points is equal to three percent of the loan amount, and so forth. Example: If you are quoted an interest rate of 7.25 percent with zero points, but you have your heart set on an interest rate of seven percent, you could pay one point and buy the interest rate down to this amount.

Yield Spread Premiums (YSP)

YSPs are rebates paid by wholesale lenders to mortgage brokers for writing loans that are above "par" or market interest rates. If the par rate is eight percent but your mortgage broker can get you to pay 8.5 percent, the wholesale lender will pay your broker an extra commission called a Yield Spread Premium. YSPs can help consumers who are short on cash. They can pay a higher interest rate and have their mortgage broker pay some of their closing costs. But mortgage brokers can make a *lot* of money with YSPs without the consumer's knowledge or consent, until the day of closing. (More on this later)

How You Can Get Ripped Off

Now let's talk about how you can get ripped off. It is tragically simple to rip off an uneducated consumer.

Closing costs

Some closing costs are legitimate fees for services performed by a third party. Your credit report and appraisal are examples of legitimate fees - some of these fees are collected up front. Some legitimate fees, (like processing fees) are collected at closing. Are all other fees junk fees? It is impossible to say. There are an endless number of ways that predatory lenders can manipulate closing costs. They can waive most of your closing costs and charge you a higher interest rate. You still pay, of course, you simply do not pay up front. They can charge you for services that are never performed. They can charge you $400 for an appraisal that costs $250.

Origination Fee

There are legitimate costs associated with loan origination and your lender is entitled to make a fair profit. To charge a one percent origination is fine, *but* to charge a one percent origination fee in conjunction with inflated or fabricated closing costs and premium interest rates could be considered excessive.

Discount points

Discount points are points paid for their stated purpose. Reducing the consumer's interest rate is a good purpose, *but* a dishonest lender can quote you a certain rate at the time of the loan application and produce something quite different at the closing table. For example, you may be told that because of a past credit problem you do not qualify for the best rate. You are "forced" to either buy down the interest rate by paying additional discount points, or you agree to a higher rate, in which case the broker receives a rebate in the form of a Yield Spread Premium, which is discussed next.

Yield Spread Premiums

If your loan officer can get you to pay a higher than market interest rate, they get a "rebate" called a Yield Spread Premium. This is how it happens. You agree to a 30-year loan at 6.5 percent. Since interest rates change daily, your loan officer will not lock in your interest rate right away. They will "float' your loan until there is a little dip in rates and then they will lock in your loan - let's say at 6.25 percent.

Since your loan officer has you committed to pay 6.5 percent, he or she will get an extra commission for selling you a loan at a higher than market interest rate. These commissions are often in the multiple thousands! An upfront and ethical loan officer would have rebated *you* the YSP or given you the 6.25 percent interest rate.

Since the lender is not required to disclose this extra profit to you until closing, you are none the wiser until it is too late to do anything about it. YSPs provide a useful option to some borrowers. For those with little cash, YSPs make no-cost mortgages possible because the lender pays closing costs. For those who expect to be in their house only a few years, YSPs permit a favorable exchange of higher rate for lower fees. *However*, in the hands of unscrupulous lenders, they can cost the borrower thousands and thousands of dollars.

How Can All This Happen?

This can all happen easily. Mortgage brokers are regulated by RESPA and other state agencies, and the good news is that positive changes have been made. Lenders can no longer charge more than three percent in fees, and they are required to disclose their profits.

But it can still be tough to enforce the rules, and even educated consumers are very easy to manipulate. The system is broken and there is no easy fix. The best thing you can do as a potential buyer is to educate yourself and hire a great Realtor to represent you.

The Lender's Dilemma

Interest rates are based on risk; the better your credentials, the lower your interest rate. Because it is a risk-based system, you will not learn your final interest rate until after you make formal loan application or until you lock your rate. It's a "chicken or the egg" scenario. Lenders don't want to commit to pricing until you make a formal loan application, and buyers don't want to commit to a loan without knowing the costs.

Closing costs are disclosed to borrowers on a document called a Good Faith Estimate (GFE). There was a time when a lender could provide a potential borrower a GFE and it was understood that the figures were just estimates. But beginning in 2010, the lender is bound by most of the fees that they quote. Because they are committed to these fees, many lenders now provide an "Initial Fees Worksheet" or a "Financing Scenario" instead of GFEs while you shop for a mortgage. By giving you this document, the lender is giving you a price without actually making a commitment.

So what does this all mean? It means that the Department of Housing and Urban Development's (HUD) recent initiatives to make shopping for a loan easier for buyers has failed, and borrowers are still going to have to take extra steps to avoid being ripped off. A lender is not necessarily a crook simply because they give you an Initial Fees Worksheet instead of a GFE; this is the policy of some of the most honest and competent lenders I know. However, it is a manipulation of the system, and the system does not make it easy for borrowers to tell the difference between the good guys and the bad guys.

How to Find a Lender

Chances are you will hear that the best place to find a lender is through a friend or family member. I disagree. Your friends and family probably have no idea if they were ripped off, and unless they work in the industry they are no match for a predatory lender. Some say that your agent is not a good resource; again I disagree. Your agent knows which lenders can close on time, which lenders deliver what they promise, and which lenders treat customers fairly. The lenders I recommend go out of their way to treat buyers well so I will continue to send them clients. Ask your agent for a list of their favorite lenders and then give them all a call, but remember that you are never required to use any vendor that your Realtor recommends.

Shopping for a Loan

After you have found a house, contact several lenders and ask for quotes. The loan officer will either refer you to their online loan application site or take information from you over the phone, and then send you either a GFE or an Initial Fees Worksheet. Compare the documents, with your agent's help if needed, and pursue the least expensive ones that can close on time. If you have a preferred lender but find their costs to be higher than some of the others, ask them to match your best deal.

This step is important. Send your top choices the following information. Do so in writing (email) with a return receipt:

- Your full name(s)
- Your monthly income(s)
- Your Social Security number(s)
- The property address
- The loan amount
- The property value or sales price

Providing them this information triggers the requirement that a GFE be delivered within three days, and also sends the message that you know what you are doing. The lender is required by RESPA (mortgage law) to give you a GFE and all the price guarantees that come along with it. Changes in income, sales price, loan program, or locking your rate can trigger a new GFE, rendering the original one obsolete. The final GFE is the one that must match your settlement statement at closing.

After comparing several GFEs, select the best loan for you and notify the loan originator that you would like to proceed with the loan. Keep your Good Faith Estimate so you can compare it with the final settlement costs stated on your HUD-1 Settlement Statement. At closing, if there are any changes in fees point them out to your lender. Some charges cannot be raised, and your lender must reimburse you if those charges were illegally increased. Others can go up by a ten percent margin, and the lender has to reimburse you for any excess.

NOTE: The loan officer may want you to give him a credit card number or a check so that he can order the appraisal. Do NOT give them a dime until you are 100 percent certain that you plan to use them. YOU ARE NOT REQUIRED TO USE A LENDER SIMPLY BECAUSE THEY SEND YOU A GOOD FAITH ESTIMATE.

Rate Shopping & Your Credit Score

Looking for a mortgage will cause multiple lenders to request your credit report, even though you are looking for only one loan. The credit scoring system ignores mortgage loan inquires made in the 30 days prior to scoring. Thus, if you find a loan within 30 days, the rate shopping will not affect your score. If you would like to play it safe, order a copy of your credit report on your own and share it with each lender with whom you request a GFE. Once you decide on a lender, you can give them permission to pull a new copy.

Points vs. Rate

When choosing a mortgage, you generally have the option to pay points (prepaid interest) in exchange for a lower interest rate. If you plan to stay in the home for more than four or five years, it is usually in your favor to pay the points. In the long run, the lower interest rate will save you more money.

Good Faith Estimate (GFE)

Let's look at a Good Faith Estimate. The information below was written by the U.S. Department of Housing and Urban Development, and offers the clearest description of the GFE that I have ever read.

The GFE is a three-page form designed to encourage you to shop for a mortgage loan and settlement services so that you can determine which mortgage is best for you. It shows the loan terms and the settlement charges you will pay if you decide to go forward with the loan process and are approved for the loan. It explains which charges can change before your settlement and which charges must remain the same. It contains a shopping chart allowing you to easily compare multiple mortgage loans and settlement costs, making it easier for you to shop for the best loan. A mortgage broker or the lender may provide the GFE. Until you let a loan originator know that you wish to proceed with a loan, the loan originator may only charge you for the cost of a credit report.

In the loan application process, the loan originator will need your name, Social Security number, gross monthly income, property address, estimate of the value of the property, and the amount of the mortgage loan you want to determine the GFE. Your Social Security number is used to obtain a credit report showing your credit history, including past and present debts and the timeliness of repayment.

Your GFE Step-by-Step

Page 1 of the GFE

Now lets go through the GFE step-by-step. The top of page 1 of the GFE shows the property address, your name and contact information and your loan originators contact information.

Important Dates

1. The interest rate for this GFE is available through [January 2, 2010 @ 4pm]. After this time, the interest rate, some of your loan Origination Charges, and the monthly payment shown below can change until you lock your interest rate.

2. This estimate for all other settlement charges is available through [January 22, 2010].

3. After you lock your interest rate, you must go to settlement within [30] days (your rate lock period) to receive the locked interest rate.

4. You must lock the interest rate at least [15] days before settlement.

The Important Dates section of the GFE includes key dates of which you should be aware.

Line 1 discloses the date and time the interest rate offer is good through.

Line 2 discloses the date All Other Settlement Charges is good through. This date must be open for at least 10 business days from the date the GFE was issued to allow you to shop for the best loan for you.

Line 3 discloses the interest rate lock time period, such as 30, 45 or 60 days, that the GFE was based on. It does not mean that your interest rate is locked.

Line 4 discloses the number of days prior to going to settlement that you must lock your interest rate.

NOTE: Locking in your rate and points at the time of application or during the processing of your loan will keep the interest rate and points from changing until the rate lock period expires.

Summary of Your Loan

Your initial loan amount is	$ 200,000.00
Your loan term is	30 years
Your initial interest rate is	5.0 %
Your initial monthly amount owed for principal, interest, and any mortgage insurance is	$ 1,173.00 per month
Can your interest rate rise?	☐ No ☒ Yes, it can rise to a maximum of %. The first change will be in
Even if you make payments on time, can your loan balance rise?	☒ No ☐ Yes, it can rise to a maximum of $
Even if you make payments on time, can your monthly amount owed for principal, interest, and any mortgage insurance rise?	☐ No ☒ Yes, the first increase can be in and the monthly amount owed can rise to $. The maximum it can ever rise to is $.
Does your loan have a prepayment penalty?	☒ No ☐ Yes, your maximum prepayment penalty is $.
Does your loan have a balloon payment?	☒ No ☐ Yes, you have a balloon payment of $ due in years.

The Summary of Your Loan Terms discloses your loan amount, loan term, the initial interest rate and the principal, interest and mortgage insurance portion of your monthly mortgage payment. It also informs you if your interest rate can increase, if your loan balance can rise, whether your mortgage payment can rise and if there is a prepayment penalty or balloon payment.

In the example above, the loan amount is $200,000, which will be paid over 30 years. The initial interest rate is 5 percent and the initial monthly mortgage payment is $1,173, which includes mortgage insurance, but does not include any amounts to pay for property taxes and homeowners insurances if required by the lender.

In our example, the loan has an adjustable interest rate. Since the interest rate can rise, the yes box was checked, and the loan originator disclosed that the initial interest rate of 5 percent could rise as high as 10 percent. The first time your interest rate could rise is 6 months after settlement, which could increase your payments to $1,290. Over the life of your loan your monthly payments could increase from $1,173 to $1,842.

This example does not contain a balloon payment or a prepayment penalty.

NOTE: A prepayment penalty is a charge that is assessed if you pay off the loan within a specified time period, such as three years. A balloon payment is due on a mortgage that usually offers a low monthly payment for an initial period of time. After that period of time elapses, the balance must be paid by the borrower, or the amount must be refinanced. You should think carefully before agreeing to these kinds of mortgage loans. If you are unable to refinance or pay the balance of the loan, you could put your home at risk.

Escrow Account Information

> Some lenders require an escrow account to hold funds for paying property taxes or other property-related charges in addition to your monthly amount owed of $ 1,173.00 .
> Do we require you to have an escrow account for your loan?
> ☐ No, you do not have an escrow account. You must pay these charges directly when due.
> ☒ Yes, you have an escrow account. It may or may not cover all of these charges. Ask us.

The GFE also includes a separate section referred to as Escrow account information, which indicates whether or not an escrow account is required. This escrow account holds funds needed to pay property taxes, homeowners insurance, flood insurance (if required by your lender) or other property-related charges. Escrows are very convenient because it spreads the cost of your property taxes and insurance over twelve monthly payments, and the bank pays the bills for you. Most lenders require an escrow account if your down payment is less than 20%.

If the GFE specifies that you will have an escrow account, you will probably have to pay an initial amount at settlement to start the account and an additional amount with each month's regular payment. If you wish to pay your property taxes and insurance directly, some lenders will give you a higher interest rate or charge you a fee. If your lender does not require an escrow account, you must pay these items directly when they are due.

Summary of Your Settlement Charges

A	Your Adjusted Origination Charges *(See page 2)*	$	3,750.00
B	Your Charges for All Other Settlement Services *(See page 2)*	$	4,530.00
A + B	Total Estimated Settlement Charges	$	8,280.00

The final section on page 1 of the GFE contains the adjusted origination charges and the total estimated charges for other settlement services, which are detailed on page 2. You should compare the Total Estimated Settlement Charges on several GFEs.

Page 2 of the GFE

The price of a home mortgage loan is stated in terms of an interest rate and settlement costs. Often, you can pay lower total settlement costs in exchange for a higher interest rate and vice versa. Ask your loan originator about different interest rates and settlement costs options.

Your Adjusted Origination Charges, Block A

Your Adjusted Origination Charges	
1. **Our origination charge** This charge is for getting this loan for you.	$6,750.00
2. **Your credit or charge (points) for the specific interest rate chosen** ☐ The credit or charge for the interest rate of [____] % is included in "Our origination charge." (See item 1 above.) ☐ You receive a credit of $ [$3,000] for this interest rate of [5%] %. This credit **reduces** your settlement charges. ☐ You pay a charge of $ [____] for this interest rate of [____] %. This charge (points) **increases** your total settlement charges. The tradeoff table on page 3 shows that you can change your total settlement charges by choosing a different interest rate for this loan.	-$3,000.00
A Your Adjusted Origination Charges	$ $3,750.00

Block 1, Our origination charge contains the lenders and the mortgage brokers charges and point(s) for originating your loan.

Block 2, Your credit or charge point(s) for the specific interest rate chosen.

If box 1 is checked, the credit or charge for the interest rate is part of the origination charge shown in Block 1.

If box 2 is checked, you will pay a higher interest rate and receive a credit to reduce your adjusted origination charge and other settlement charges.

If box 3 is checked, you will be paying point(s) to reduce your interest rate and, therefore, will pay higher adjusted origination charges.

Note: A point is equal to one percent of your loan amount.

After adding or subtracting Block 2 from Block 1, Your Adjusted Origination Charge is shown in Block A.

In the example shown, the origination charge is $6,750. No points were paid to reduce the interest rate. Instead, because of the interest rate chosen, the offer contains a $3,000 credit that reduces the adjusted origination charge to $3,750.

Your Charges for All Other Settlement Services, Blocks 3 through 11

3. **Required services that we select** These charges are for services we require to complete your settlement. We will choose the providers of these services. *Service* — *Charge* Appraisal — $275.00 Flood Certification — $52.00 Tax Service — $56.00	$383.00
4. **Title services and lender's title insurance** This charge includes the services of a title or settlement agent, for example, and title insurance to protect the lender, if required.	$1,275.00
5. **Owner's title insurance** You may purchase an owner's title insurance policy to protect your interest in the property.	$175.00
6. **Required services that you can shop for** These charges are for other services that are required to complete your settlement. We can identify providers of these services or you can shop for them yourself. Our estimates for providing these services are below. *Service* — *Charge* Survey — $250.00 Pest Inspection — $45.00	$295.00

In addition to the charges to originate your loan, there are other charges for services that will be required to get your mortgage. For some of the services, the loan originator will choose the company that performs the service (Block 3). The loan originator usually permits you to select the settlement service provider for Title services and lenders title insurance (Block 4). Owners title insurance is also disclosed (Block 5). Other required services that you may shop for are included in Required Services that you can shop for (Block 6).

Block 3 contains charges for required services for which the loan originator selects the settlement service provider. These are not shoppable services and often include items such as the property appraisal, credit report, flood certification, tax service and any required mortgage insurance.

Block 4 contains the charge for title services, the Lenders title insurance policy and the services of a title, settlement or escrow agent to conduct your settlement.

Block 5 contains the charge for an Owners title insurance policy that protects your interests.

NOTE: Under RESPA, the seller may not require you, as a condition of the sale, to purchase title insurance from any particular title company.

7. Government recording charges These charges are for state and local fees to record your loan and title documents.	$50.00
8. Transfer taxes These charges are for state and local fees on mortgages and home sales.	$1,368.00
9. Initial deposit for your escrow account This charge is held in an escrow account to pay future recurring charges on your property and includes [x] all property taxes, [x] all insurance, and [ ] other [ ].	$306.00
10. Daily interest charges This charge is for the daily interest on your loan from the day of your settlement until the first day of the next month or the first day of your normal mortgage payment cycle. This amount is $[28.00] per day for [1] days (if your settlement is [1/31/2010]).	$28.00
11. Homeowner's insurance This charge is for the insurance you must buy for the property to protect from a loss, such as fire. Policy Charge Homeowner's insurance $650.00	$650.00

Block 6 contains charges for required services for which you may shop for the provider. Some of these items may include a survey or pest inspection.

Block 7 contains charges by governmental entities to record the deed and documents related to the loan.

Block 8 contains charges by state and local governments for taxes related to the mortgage and transferring title to the property.

Block 9 contains the initial amount you will pay at settlement to start the escrow account, if required by the lender.

Block 10 contains the charge for the daily interest on the loan from the day of settlement to the first day of the following month.

Block 11 contains the annual charge for any insurance the lender requires to protect the property such as homeowners insurance and flood insurance.

Total Estimated Settlement Charges

B	Your Charges for All Other Settlement Services	$ $4,530
A + B	Total Estimated Settlement Charges	$ $8,280

"Your charges for All Other Settlement Services", Blocks 3 through 11, are totaled in Block B. Blocks A and B are added together resulting in the total estimated settlement charges associated with getting the loan. These Blocks are carried forward to the bottom of page 1 of the GFE.

Page 3 of the GFE

Page 3 of the GFE contains important instructions and information that will help you shop for the best loan for you.

Understanding Which Charges Can Change at Settlement

These charges cannot increase at settlement:	The total of these charges can increase up to 10% at settlement:	These charges can change at settlement:
■ Our origination charge	■ Required services that we select	■ Required services that you can shop for (if you do not use companies we identify)
■ Your credit or charge (points) for the specific interest rate chosen (after you lock in your interest rate)	■ Title services and lender's title insurance (if we select them or you use companies we identify)	■ Title services and lender's title insurance (if you do not use companies we identify)
■ Your adjusted origination charges (after you lock in your interest rate)	■ Owner's title insurance (if you use companies we identify)	■ Owner's title insurance (if you do not use companies we identify)
■ Transfer taxes	■ Required services that you can shop for (if you use companies we identify)	■ Initial deposit for your escrow account
	■ Government recording charges	■ Daily interest charges
		■ Homeowner's insurance

There are three different categories of charges that you will pay at closing: charges that cannot increase at settlement; charges that cannot increase in total more than 10%; and charges that can increase at settlement. You can use this as a guide to understand which charges can or cannot change. Compare your GFE to the actual charges listed on the HUD-1 Settlement Statement to ensure that your lender is not charging you more than permitted.

Written List of Settlement Service Providers

A written list will be given to you with your GFE that includes all settlement services that you are required to have and that you are allowed to shop for. You may select a provider from this list or you can choose your own qualified provider. If you choose a name from the written list provided, that charge is within the 10% tolerance category. If you select your own service provider, the 10% tolerance will not apply.

Even though you may find a better deal by selecting your own provider, you should choose the provider carefully as those charges could increase at settlement. If your loan originator fails to provide a list of settlement service providers, the 10% tolerance automatically applies.

Using the Tradeoff Table

	The loan in this GFE	The same loan with lower settlement charges	The same loan with a lower interest rate
Your initial loan amount	$ 200,000.00	$ 200,000.00	$ 200,000.00
Your initial interest rate[1]	5 %	6 %	4.5 %
Your initial monthly amount owed	$	$	$
Change in the monthly amount owed from this GFE	No change	You will pay $ more every month	You will pay $ less every month
Change in the amount you will pay at settlement with this interest rate	No change	Your settlement charges will be reduced by $ 1,500	Your settlement charges will increase by $ 1,500
How much your total estimated settlement charges will be	$ 8,280.00	$ 6,780.00	$ 9,780.00

[1] For an adjustable rate loan, the comparisons above are for the initial interest rate before adjustments are made.

The tradeoff table on page 3 will help you understand how your loan payments can change if you pay more settlement charges and receive a lower interest rate or if you pay lower settlement charges and receive a higher interest rate.

Using the Shopping Chart

	This loan	Loan 2	Loan 3	Loan 4
Loan originator name	ABC Company	DEF Company	CS Company	
Initial loan amount	$200,000.00	$200,000.00	$200,000.00	
Loan term	30 Years	30 Years	30 Years	
Initial interest rate	5.0%	5.0%	5.375%	
Initial monthly amount owed	$1,173.00	$1,173.00	$1,219.00	
Rate lock period	30 Days	30 Days	30 Days	
Can interest rate rise?	yes	yes	yes	
Can loan balance rise?	no	no	no	
Can monthly amount owed rise?	yes	yes	yes	
Prepayment penalty?	no	no	no	
Balloon payment?	no	no	no	
Total Estimated Settlement Charges	$8,280.00	$8,309.00	$5,480.00	

You can use this chart to compare similar loans offered by different loan originators. Fill in each column with the information shown in the Summary of your loan section from the first page of all the GFEs you receive. Compare each offer and select the best loan for you.

The loan originator must complete the first column with information contained in the GFE. If the loan originator has the same loan product available with a higher or lower interest rate, the loan originator may choose to complete the remaining columns. If the second and third columns are not filled in, ask your loan originator if they have the same loan product with different interest rates.

Types of Loans

Conventional vs. FHA Financing

Over the past few years, subprime and no money down financing programs have disappeared, and the mortgage industry has gone back to traditional mortgage programs. FHA and Conventional financing are the most traditional type of financing. If you can qualify for conventional financing, it is the least expensive option. If not, pursue an FHA. Some people mistakenly believe that FHA loans are strictly for low-income borrowers. This is absolutely not true. People of all incomes obtain FHA loans.

FHA Financing

FHA is a government insured mortgage program, meaning the government guarantees the loan if the borrower defaults. This type of financing was part of the government's initiative to encourage homeownership. The FHA program is becoming more and more popular lately, since it is easier to qualify for than a conventional mortgage. FHA is, however, a little more expensive than conventional financing. The minimum down payment on an FHA loan is 3.5 percent of the purchase price, and they do accept gifted funds from a close relative. The credit requirements are much more relaxed, and you can usually get a loan with a 640 credit score. If you have a larger down payment or larger reserves, you can sometimes qualify with even a lower credit score.

Mortgage insurance is an insurance policy that protects lenders in the event a borrower defaults on the loan. FHA loans requires two different types of mortgage insurance premiums for most buyers. The first is called the Upfront Mortgage Insurance Premium (UFMIP), and is a percentage (approximately 1.5 percent) of the total amount that you are borrowing. It can be paid in cash at closing, or can be rolled into the loan amount. The second type of mortgage insurance is called monthly Mortgage Insurance (MI). FHA Mortgage Insurance will need to be in place until you have 20 percent equity in your property, but for a minimum of five years.

Conventional Financing

Conventional mortgages are for those borrowers with higher scores and more asset reserves. Credit scores for conventional mortgages need to be in the 680 plus range. Expect to put down between 5 percent and sometimes 10 percent when you purchase a home using a conventional mortgage. First time buyers with excellent credit profiles will be able to put down as little as 5 percent. Monthly Mortgage insurance only applies if you are putting less than 20 percent down. If you are putting 20 percent or more down, there will be no monthly mortgage insurance.

Fixed Rate vs. Adjustable

Fixed rate or adjustable refers to the interest rate, which can either remain the same throughout the life of the loan, or change periodically. Fixed and adjustable rates are discussed below.

Fixed Rate

A fixed rate mortgage has an interest rate that never changes. This means, unlike an adjustable rate mortgage, you are protected from higher monthly mortgage payments if interest rates suddenly rise. If mortgage rates drop, however, you do not benefit from the lower rate unless you refinance.

Even though the interest rate is fixed, the amount that you will pay depends on the mortgage term. The most common terms are 30, 20, and 15 years. The 30-year mortgage is the most popular because it has the lowest monthly payment. The trade off is that the loan overall costs a lot more because you are paying extra interest for ten or fifteen years. Additionally, the interest rate of a 30-year mortgage is typically higher than with a shorter term.

If you're interested in a shorter-term loan but are concerned about the higher payment, go with the 30-year mortgage, and follow the advice in the section titled "Prepaying Your Mortgage" later in the book.

Adjustable Rate Mortgages

ARMs are attractive to some because the initial rate is low, which allows the borrower to qualify for a larger loan. They are risky because your mortgage interest rate (and therefore your mortgage payment) changes frequently over the life of the loan. Some are structured so that interest rates can more than double in just a few years. If you are don't plan to live in a property long enough for the rates to rise, than an ARM might be a good choice. Otherwise, and especially given today's low interest rates, stick with a Fixed Rate Mortgage.

Your Loan Step-by-Step

The following is a description of what happens, step-by-step, after you choose a lender and complete your loan application:

1. Documentation is Ordered - Within twenty-four hours of application, your lender will order a credit report, appraisal, verifications of employment and funds to close, and any other supporting documentation that is necessary.

2. Wait for Documentation - After you submit your supporting documentation, the loan officer checks for any potential problems and requests additional items as needed. It can take two or three weeks for all the items to be received.

3. Loan Submission - Once all the necessary documentation is in, the loan officer reviews the current programs to ensure you get the best rate and terms possible. The loan processor then puts the loan package together and submits it to the underwriter for approval.

4. Loan Approval - Loan approval generally takes anywhere from 24 to 72 hours. All parties are notified of the approval and any loan conditions that must be received before the loan can close. The loan approval is the beginning of the closing process.

5. Documents are Created - Within one to three days after the loan approval, the loan documents (including the note and deed of trust) are completed and sent to the title company. The escrow officer calls the borrowers to come in when the papers are ready for final signature. At this time, the borrowers are told how much money they will need to bring in to close the loan.

6. Funding - Once all parties have signed the loan documents, they are returned to the lender who reviews the package. If all the forms have been properly executed, the check is issued to fund the loan.

7. Recording - When the title company receives the funding check from the lender, they make the lender's security for the loan a matter of public record. They do this by recording the note and deed of trust at the county recorder's office. Escrow is now officially closed and the house is yours!

CHAPTER SEVEN
A Moment of Silence

After repairs have been agreed upon and you have made a formal loan application with your lender, things can get very quiet. Some buyers mistakenly believe that nothing is happening, when in fact there are many, many things taking place behind the scenes. All the following items below must be completed and approved before closing:

Title Insurance

Title insurance is protection against loss arising from problems connected with the title to your property. Before you purchased your home, several people may have owned the property, and even more may have owned the land. This is called the "chain of title." When the property sold, if someone forged a signature (perhaps a former spouse), or if there were unpaid taxes or other liens, there is a cloud on the title. A cloud on the title indicates that there is a lien or claim that needs to be cleared before it can be sold.

Title insurance covers the insured party for any claims and legal fees that arise from such issues. If you buy a house, for example, and someone's former spouse claims that he or she never signed the paperwork to sell the house, you are covered by title insurance. The lender required insurance protects the lender up to the amount of the mortgage, but it doesn't protect your equity in the property. For that you need an owner's title policy for the full value of the home. In many areas, sellers pay for owner policies as part of their obligation to deliver good title to the buyer. In other areas, borrowers must buy it as an add-on to the lender policy.

Appraisal

An appraiser, an objective third party to the transaction, performs the appraisal. The appraiser's job is to give their professional opinion of the market value of a home. Lenders use the appraisal to determine the appropriate loan amount. A lender will not lend more than the value of the home, and the appraised value is used to determine common loan ratios that factor into the loan approval process, such as loan to value, or LTV. You are entitled to a copy of the appraisal; after all you paid $350-400 for it. If your lender does not send you a copy on their own, ask them for it. They are required to give it to you.

Survey

A property survey is a sketch or map of a property showing its boundaries and other physical features (see below). They also show the relative location of a house, shed, other building and fences on the property, and it usually includes the position of any public or municipal easements. Mortgage lenders generally require a property survey before they will loan money for a mortgage, and many title insurers require this as well. Some states, like Texas, allow the sellers to share their survey with the buyer, assuming there have been no changes to the property. This saves the buyer several hundred dollars at closing.

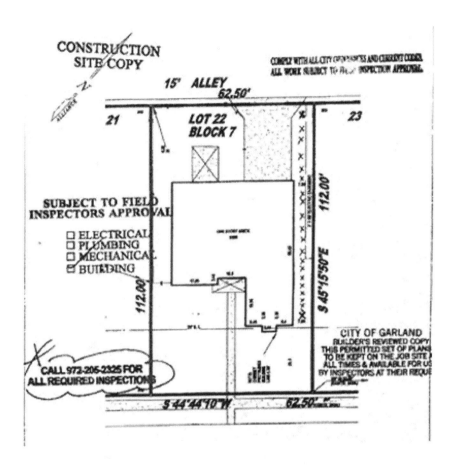

COMPLY WITH ALL CITY ORDINANCES AND CURRENT CODES.
ALL WORK SUBJECT TO FIELD INSPECTION APPROVAL.

15' ALLEY
62.50'

21   23

LOT 22
BLOCK 7

112.00'

S 45°15'50"E

SUBJECT TO FIELD
INSPECTORS APPROVAL

☐ ELECTRICAL
☐ PLUMBING
☐ MECHANICAL
☑ BUILDING

112.00'

CITY OF GARLAND
BUILDER'S REVIEWED COPY
THIS PERMITTED SET OF PLANS
TO BE KEPT ON THE JOB SITE
ALL TIMES & AVAILABLE FOR US
BY INSPECTORS AT THEIR REQUE

CALL 973-205-2325 FOR
ALL REQUIRED INSPECTIONS

S 44°44'10"W   62.50'

117

Loan Approval

The steps of the loan process were discussed earlier. To recap, after you turn in all your supporting documents, your loan is turned over to the underwriter for final approval. After all the underwriter's conditions are met, your file is declared "clear to close." The documents are then prepared and sent to the title company.

Homeowner's Association (HOA)

If you are buying in a neighborhood with an HOA, the association will be notified, and the paperwork will be transferred to your name. If the seller has any outstanding fees or fines, they will be collected prior to closing. After closing you'll receive an invoice directly from the HOA when the next year's fees are due.

Homeowner's Insurance

It is your responsibility to obtain homeowner's insurance before closing. Homeowner's insurance protects a homeowner against loss from fire and other hazards that may impair the value of their home. It is a lot easier to shop for homeowner's insurance than a mortgage because premiums change only occasionally, so the price you are quoted is very likely the price you will pay.

In shopping for the lowest premium, you need to be very careful to compare apples with apples. You need to compare two items: the deductible and the coverage.

The "deductible" is the loss that is the homeowner's responsibility. Only losses above that amount are insured. Higher deductibles carry lower premiums. But lenders limit the amount of deductible they will allow – one percent is a typical maximum.

The "coverage" dictates the maximum loss the policy will pay. There are four levels of coverage:

- actual cash value (lowest coverage)
- replacement cost
- extended replacement cost
- guaranteed replacement cost (highest coverage, but not necessarily available).

Higher coverage carries higher premiums. Lenders typically require coverage of 125 percent of the cost of replacement, though this may be scaled down if the land accounts for an unusually large part of the house value.

Call several insurance agents for quotes, and when you have made your selection you can have the insurance agent send a "binder" to the title company. The title company is responsible for collecting money from you and paying for the policy at closing.

Home Warranty

A home warranty is a contract between a home warranty company and a homeowner that provides discounted repair or replacement on a variety of items in a home. You can choose your level of coverage to include the basic items like the furnace, air conditioning, plumbing, and electrical systems, or you can add coverage for appliances, pools, refrigerators, and others.

If something in your house that was working at closing breaks, you call the home warranty company. The home warranty sends over the right service provider for the job. The repair is made or the component is replaced, and the homeowner only pays the cost of the service call, usually $60-80.

There are many different home warranty companies and many different levels of service. There are varied exclusions in their contracts, so review them carefully when you make your selection, and match the right coverage to the house you are buying. For example, if the water heater works but is a little dated, be sure that the policy you pick will replace it.

I always negotiate a home warranty for my buyer/clients (except for new homes), and so should you unless the home you are buying is in pristine condition and everything is new.

CHAPTER EIGHT
Walk-Throughs & Lease Backs

Pre-Closing Walk-Through

A walk-through is a final inspection of the home before closing, and I recommend two of them. The first should be done forty-eight hours before closing to verify that all the agreed upon repairs have been completed (get receipts!), and to make sure that there hasn't been any damage to the property since you were last there. You do not want to wait until an hour before closing to express dissatisfaction with the condition of the home since the seller needs time to make corrections. Take your camera and take pictures of anything wrong with the property, and let your agent share them with the seller's side.

The second walk-through should be done immediately before closing, just to be sure everything is okay before you sign your papers. This is something I generally do for my buyers since they are busy at the bank and often are coming right from work.

If something *major* is wrong with the house, don't close. "Major" means something big like the air conditioner doesn't work, the house was vandalized, there was a hailstorm that damaged the roof, and other similar conditions. *The house needs to be turned over to you in the condition it was in at inspection, including the agreed upon repairs, or you do not close.*

If you have small grievances, your agent can negotiate money for you to make the repair after closing, or the title company can hold back some of the seller's proceeds in escrow until the situation has been resolved. It is during times like this that you need a good agent to represent your interests.

Temporary Lease Backs

Quite often, the seller does not move out of the property until after closing and funding. It's risky for them to leave until they are 100 percent certain the deal will close. For the period of time after funding when the buyer officially owns the house, to the time that the seller moves out, the seller is living in the buyer's house. You absolutely must have the sellers sign a temporary lease agreement, which means they are your tenants until they move out. With a proper lease, the seller can be evicted if they refuse to move out.

Make certain the lease specifies that the house needs to be left in clean, move-in condition. The word "clean" is subjective, of course. I generally suggest that buyers plan on hiring a cleaning service and carpet cleaners before they move in, and to consider it a closing cost. You might get lucky and the seller will leave you a spotless house, but I doubt it.

CHAPTER NINE
Closing

The closing is when all the paperwork is signed and when all funds are disbursed. A title company or settlement company facilitates the entire process. The title company is also the issuer of your title insurance policy. As a mostly neutral third party to the transaction, the settlement company has many responsibilities including:

- Cashing the buyer's earnest money check and holding the money in a trust account
- Managing the paperwork between the buyer's agent and the seller's agent, the lender, insurance companies, and home warranty providers.
- Coordinating the funding of the loan
- Paying off the seller's loan
- Preparing the HUD-1 closing cost settlement statement
- Disbursing the seller's checks and the agent's commissions
- Prorating annual property taxes and other obligations

Once your loan is fully approved and you are clear to close, your lender will send papers and instructions to the title/settlement company. Based on those instructions, the closer will prepare your closing statement and distribute it to all the parties involved for approval. You can compare your Good Faith Estimate to the actual closing statement to see how close your lender's estimate was to actual figures. If there are any big surprises, discuss them with your agent and lender immediately. Also be certain that you received a credit for any deposits you put down for earnest money, any option fees, prepaid appraisals, and so forth. Again, your agent should be extremely familiar with this document and can help you. You will need to bring a cashier's check in the appropriate amount to closing; be sure to keep your funds readily accessible in a local account.

Once approved, both buyer and seller will sign the documents, and the funds will be distributed to the appropriate parties. When everyone has been paid, you get the keys to your new house!

HUD 1 - Closing Statement

The closing agent will prepare a HUD-1 prior to your closing, and it must be given to the borrower at least one day prior to your closing date (in reality, this doesn't always happen). The final version will state all costs involved with the loan and to whom charges will be paid. A sample closing and explanation of each section follows:

Sections B through H

Sections B through H cover basic information about the transaction, including the name and address of the parties involved, and the name and address of the title company. Pay attention to the loan type. If you are getting an FHA but the box is checked for a conventional loan, mention in to the closer.

Summaries of Borrower's and Seller's Transactions

Section J summarizes the buyer's costs. The numbers in the 100 series are funds due from the buyer. Line 120 is the total amount due. The 200 series are buyer credits; line 220 is the total amount of buyer credits. Be certain that you receive credit for your earnest money and any option fee you may have paid. Line 301 is simply the amount in line 120. Line 302 is the amount in line 220. When line 302 is subtracted from line 301, the amount that you need to bring to closing is the result, and is listed in line 303. You'll need to either wire the money to the title company or get certified funds. Section K is the Seller's side. Some states require that this side be blank on the buyer's copy.

OMB Approval No. 2502-0265

A. Settlement Statement (HUD-1)

B. Type of Loan

1. ☐ FHA	2. ☐ RHS	3. ☐ Conv. Unins.	6. File Number:	7. Loan Number:	8. Mortgage Insurance Case Number:
4. ☐ VA	5. ☐ Conv. Ins.				

D. Name & Address of Borrower:	E. Name & Address of Seller:	F. Name & Address of Lender:
G. Property Location:	H. Settlement Agent:	I. Settlement Date:
	Place of Settlement:	

J. Summary of Borrower's Transaction

100. Gross Amount Due from Borrower	
101. Contract sales price	
102. Personal property	
103. Settlement charges to borrower (line 1400)	
104.	
105.	
Adjustment for items paid by seller in advance	
106. City/town taxes to	
107. County taxes to	
108. Assessments to	
109.	
110.	
111.	
112.	
120. Gross Amount Due from Borrower	
200. Amount Paid by or in Behalf of Borrower	
201. Deposit or earnest money	
202. Principal amount of new loan(s)	
203. Existing loan(s) taken subject to	
204.	
205.	
206.	
207.	
208.	
209.	
Adjustments for items unpaid by seller	
210. City/town taxes to	
211. County taxes to	
212. Assessments to	
213.	
214.	
215.	
216.	
217.	
218.	
219.	
220. Total Paid by/for Borrower	
300. Cash at Settlement from/to Borrower	
301. Gross amount due from borrower (line 120)	
302. Less amounts paid by/for borrower (line 220)	( )
303. Cash ☐ From ☐ To Borrower	

K. Summary of Seller's Transaction

400. Gross Amount Due to Seller	
401. Contract sales price	
402. Personal property	
403.	
404.	
405.	
Adjustment for items paid by seller in advance	
406. City/town taxes to	
407. County taxes to	
408. Assessments to	
409.	
410.	
411.	
412.	
420. Gross Amount Due to Seller	
500. Reductions in Amount Due to seller	
501. Excess deposit (see instructions)	
502. Settlement charges to seller (line 1400)	
503. Existing loan(s) taken subject to	
504. Payoff of first mortgage loan	
505. Payoff of second mortgage loan	
506.	
507.	
508.	
509.	
Adjustments for items unpaid by seller	
510. City/town taxes to	
511. County taxes to	
512. Assessments to	
513.	
514.	
515.	
516.	
517.	
518.	
519.	
520. Total Reduction Amount Due Seller	
600. Cash at Settlement to/from Seller	
601. Gross amount due to seller (line 420)	
602. Less reductions in amounts due seller (line 520)	( )
603. Cash ☐ To ☐ From Seller	

Settlement Charges

This section, on Page 2, contains the 700 series of real estate brokerage fees, 800 series of lender fees, 900 series of prepaid charges (such as interest and mortgage insurance), 1000 series of escrow (or impound) deposits, 1100 series of title insurance fees, 1200 series of government recording fees and transfer taxes, and 1300 series of other settlement charges. The last is a catchall used for such miscellaneous expenses as a home inspection or pest control report.

L. Settlement Charges

700. Total Real Estate Broker Fees		Paid From Borrower's Funds at Settlement	Paid From Seller's Funds at Settlement
Division of commission (line 700) as follows:			
701. $ to			
702. $ to			
703. Commission paid at settlement			
704.			

800. Items Payable in Connection with Loan				
801. Our origination charge	$	(from GFE #1)		
802. Your credit or charge (points) for the specific interest rate chosen	$	(from GFE #2)		
803. Your adjusted origination charges		(from GFE #A)		
804. Appraisal fee to		(from GFE #3)		
805. Credit report to		(from GFE #3)		
806. Tax service to		(from GFE #3)		
807. Flood certification to		(from GFE #3)		
808.				
809.				
810.				
811.				

900. Items Required by Lender to be Paid in Advance				
901. Daily interest charges from to @ $ /day		(from GFE #10)		
902. Mortgage insurance premium for months to		(from GFE #3)		
903. Homeowner's insurance for years to		(from GFE #11)		
904.				

1000. Reserves Deposited with Lender				
1001. Initial deposit for your escrow account		(from GFE #9)		
1002. Homeowner's insurance months @ $ per month $				
1003. Mortgage insurance months @ $ per month $				
1004. Property Taxes months @ $ per month $				
1005. months @ $ per month $				
1006. months @ $ per month $				
1007. Aggregate Adjustment -$				

1100. Title Charges				
1101. Title services and lender's title insurance		(from GFE #4)		
1102. Settlement or closing fee	$			
1103. Owner's title insurance		(from GFE #5)		
1104. Lender's title insurance	$			
1105. Lender's title policy limit $				
1106. Owner's title policy limit $				
1107. Agent's portion of the total title insurance premium to	$			
1108. Underwriter's portion of the total title insurance premium to	$			
1109.				
1110.				
1111.				

1200. Government Recording and Transfer Charges				
1201. Government recording charges		(from GFE #7)		
1202. Deed $ Mortgage $ Release $				
1203. Transfer taxes		(from GFE #8)		
1204. City/County tax/stamps Deed $ Mortgage $				
1205. State tax/stamps Deed $ Mortgage $				
1206.				

1300. Additional Settlement Charges				
1301. Required services that you can shop for		(from GFE #6)		
1302. $				
1303. $				
1304.				
1305.				

1400. Total Settlement Charges (enter on lines 103, Section J and 502, Section K)			

Comparison of Good Faith Estimate (GFE) and HUD-1 Charges

Page 3 compares what you were quoted on your Good Faith Estimate with your actual loan charges on your HUD-1. You can see a line-by-line comparison of the estimated and actual costs. The total, shown at the bottom of the second chart, shows the difference between the GFE and HUD-1 in both dollars and percentages. The costs cannot increase by more than ten percent; if they do, a refund must be issued to the buyer to cover the overage.

Comparison of Good Faith Estimate (GFE) and HUD-1 Charges		Good Faith Estimate	HUD-1
Charges That Cannot Increase	HUD-1 Line Number		
Our origination charge	# 801		
Your credit or charge (points) for the specific interest rate chosen	# 802		
Your adjusted origination charges	# 803		
Transfer taxes	# 1203		

Charges That In Total Cannot Increase More Than 10%		Good Faith Estimate	HUD-1
Government recording charges	# 1201		
	#		
	#		
	#		
	#		
	#		
	#		
Total			
Increase between GFE and HUD-1 Charges		$ or	%

Charges That Can Change		Good Faith Estimate	HUD-1
Initial deposit for your escrow account	# 1001		
Daily interest charges $ /day	# 901		
Homeowner's insurance	# 903		
	#		
	#		
	#		

Loan Terms

Your initial loan amount is	$
Your loan term is	years
Your initial interest rate is	%
Your initial monthly amount owed for principal, interest, and any mortgage insurance is	$ Includes ☐ Principal ☐ Interest ☐ Mortgage Insurance
Can your interest rate rise?	☐ No ☐ Yes, it can rise to a maximum of %. The first change will be on and can change again every after Every change date, your interest rate can increase or decrease by %. Over the life of the loan, your interest rate is guaranteed to never be **lower** than % or **higher** than %
Even if you make payments on time, can your loan balance rise?	☐ No ☐ Yes, it can rise to a maximum of $
Even if you make payments on time, can your monthly amount owed for principal, interest, and mortgage insurance rise?	☐ No ☐ Yes, the first increase can be on and the monthly amount owed can rise to $. The maximum it can ever rise to is $
Does your loan have a prepayment penalty?	☐ No ☐ Yes, your maximum prepayment penalty is $
Does your loan have a balloon payment?	☐ No ☐ Yes, you have a balloon payment of $ due in years on
Total monthly amount owed including escrow account payments	☐ You do not have a monthly escrow payment for items, such as property taxes and homeowner's insurance. You must pay these items directly yourself. ☐ You have an additional monthly escrow payment of $ that results in a total initial monthly amount owed of $. This includes principal, interest, any mortgage insurance and any items checked below: ☐ Property taxes ☐ Homeowner's insurance ☐ Flood insurance ☐ ☐

Note: If you have any questions about the Settlement Charges and Loan Terms listed on this form, please contact your lender.

133

Loan Terms

The final section recaps the terms of the loan, including the loan amount, interest rate, monthly payment of principal, interest and mortgage insurance, if any, and loan term. The terms of the loan are recapped and you can verify whether or not the interest rate can rise, whether there is a prepayment penalty or a balloon payment. A sample HUD-1 is pictured below. Be absolutely certain that you receive credit for every check you wrote outside of closing. If you paid for something outside of closing (like a credit report or appraisal), it should be listed on the HUD statement with POC (paid outside closing) next to it.

At the Closing Table

You will be asked to sign a huge stack of papers at the closing table. The ones that need to concern you are:

- HUD-1 Closing Statement – As discussed earlier, be sure the figures are accurate.
- Note – This is your promise to pay back the loan to the mortgage company. Be absolutely sure that the interest rate, term, etc., are correct.
- Deed of Trust –If you don't pay, you don't get to stay. This document describes how they will confiscate the house if you are delinquent.
- IRS Documents – On any IRS related document, be certain that your social security number is correct so that you can deduct the mortgage interest from your taxes.
- Make sure your Temporary Lease is in order.

All the rest of the documents are usually fluff. At closing, you'll receive copies of everything you signed, your survey, and home warranty information. Your agent will make arrangements to deliver your keys after funding.

CHAPTER TEN
After the Sale

Recording Process

The recording process is the final step in the closing process. The closing company, attorney, or title company that handles your transaction will complete the recording. The process officially records certain documents such as the warranty deed and the security instrument.

Meeting Your New Financial Obligations

You should have received a payment coupon for your first house payment at closing. Do not be surprised if you receive a letter from the lender telling you that the loan has been sold. This is a very common practice. The lender will tell you where to mail your payments if your loan was sold, and you should receive a coupon booklet in the mail from the new lender, which is now your loan servicer. Even if you do not receive a payment coupon, you need to make your payments on time. Contact the loan servicer for payment information.

The loan servicer will keep track of your payment history and will apply your monthly loan payment to the balance and escrow reserves. The loan servicer is responsible for paying your real estate taxes and hazard insurance from the escrow reserves. While the tax and insurance bills *should* go directly to the loan servicer, they *may* come to you. If so, just forward them to the servicer for payment. Your payment may increase in the future if a higher escrow balance is needed to meet rising real estate tax or insurance costs. The loan servicer will provide a year-end interest statement and account analysis so that you can monitor this. You will also need this information when you file your taxes to ensure you take the appropriate deductions for the interest and real estate taxes you have paid. Consult your tax adviser with any questions.

Homestead Exemptions

A homestead exemption reduces the value of a home for state and local tax purposes. Once you file the appropriate paperwork with your local tax office, you are eligible for a sizable discount on your property taxes. Almost all states have some type of exemption; the amounts and filing requirements vary from state to state. Ask your Realtor for more information, or contact your local tax office for instructions on how to file.

Prepaying Your Mortgage

Prepaying part of your mortgage allows you to pay a lot less in interest. For every extra dollar you apply toward your loan principal, you save about two dollars in interest. For example, on a $200,000 loan with a five percent interest rate, paying an extra $50/month will save you almost $21,000 over the life of the loan, and the loan term will be reduced by almost three years. That means your 30-year loan becomes a 27-year loan. The same result can be obtained by making one extra mortgage payment a year. If you decide to prepay your mortgage, don't sign up for the "bi-weekly prepayment program" that your lender will offer you. These programs require that you pay a set up fee of about $300-400, plus a $5-8 per month service charge. You can almost always prepay at no charge. Just add the extra amount to your normal monthly payment, or pay the extra amount separately so it is easier to audit later.

Cancelling PMI

There are two ways to get rid of your PMI. First, you can request cancellation once you pay down your mortgage to the point where you have 20 percent equity. For example, if your original loan amount was $100,000, your loan balance needs to be $80,000 before you can cancel it.

The other way is automatic cancellation by the lender when you have 22 percent equity in your home. Clearly it makes more sense and it will save you money to request cancellation at 20 percent rather than waiting for the automatic cancellation. Contact your lender to determine their procedures for canceling your PMI.

Here Come The Scams!

When you buy a house, the deed is recorded with the county and becomes public record. Businesses create mailing lists of people who just bought a home, and try to sell them things. The junk mail is endless! On the plus side, you do receive lots of valuable coupons to furniture stores, home improvement centers, and many other retail establishments, so keep you eyes open for those! Also, look out for the following scams:

Homestead Scams

Filing your homestead exemption is free. Scammers will send you very official looking documents with filing instructions, and charge you $25-$50 to record the document for you. Don't fall for this one! Just go online to your county's appraisal district and look for filing instructions. Some counties even let you file your exemption online.

Mortgage Scams

We've already discussed the benefits of making biweekly mortgage payments, or paying a little extra with your normal monthly payment. You don't have to pay your mortgage company or any other company to do this; you can make the extra payment for free at any time. I recommend sending a separate check (or second online payment) and specify in the memo field that it be applied toward "principal only." Be on the lookout for companies that try to get you to send them your mortgage payment, claiming that they will make your payment for you. If you ever get a letter stating that your loan was sold or transferred to another bank, and that you should start sending your payments to a different address, call the old bank and verify this information before you send any money.

Mortgage Insurance

After closing, you'll start receiving offers from numerous insurance companies. The policy they try to sell you is one that makes your house payment for you if you die or become disabled. You are generally better off buying a normal term life policy and/or disability insurance. These policies are overpriced and sometimes underwritten by less than reputable insurance companies. What good is insurance if the company is bankrupt when you need it?

Predatory Refinancing

Refinancing your home can help reduce monthly payments and is a great financial planning tool when it is used responsibly and properly. It costs several thousand dollars to refinance your home, and those who make a habit of refinancing can very quickly end up owing far more than the house is worth.

When borrowers refinance their homes repeatedly to take out all of their equity, it is called equity stripping. While there are legitimate reasons to cash out the equity in your home, it is important for your financial future to build equity in your home.

Foreclosure "Rescue" Scams

If you are having problems making your mortgage payment, contact your lender as quickly as possible and see what options they offer. Definitely avoid any business that:

- Provide a money back guarantee that says they can stop the foreclosure
- Advises you not to contact your lender
- Tries to collect a fee from you
- Only accepts a cashier's check or wire transfer
- Advises you to make your mortgage payment directly to them
- Tries to get you to transfer your title

Contracts for Deed

A contract for deed is often called "rent to own" financing, and is commonly used with seller financed transactions. Under a contract for deed, the property title remains in the name of the seller until the buyer has made a certain number of payments, and sometimes until after he or she has paid off the house completely. Although the seller is supposed to transfer the title to the buyer after they have paid off the house, this doesn't always happen. Basically, the buyers are paying for a house that they very often will never really own. Contracts for deed are a great deal for the seller, but are a nightmare for the buyer.

CHAPTER ELEVEN
What Can Go Wrong

In homebuying, much can go wrong. Besides your Realtor, at least 15-20 other professionals are involved in a real estate transaction, and while they all have the same goal in mind, things happen that delay closing or forfeit the sale. Here are some examples:

- The survey shows an encroachment or other problem
- The lender cannot clear the borrower's loan conditions in time
- The buyer creates a problem with his credit by opening new lines of credit or switching jobs
- Hail, wind, fire, vandals, etc., damage the property.
- The title search finds a lien against the property, and the seller does not have the cash to clear it
- During the final walk through, new damage or theft is discovered, or the seller removed things from the home that were supposed to stay.
- The title company does not receive documents in time for closing
- Seller changes their mind or refuses to move
- Seller is buying a new home and there is a problem with that transaction
- Seller dies
- There is a hailstorm between inspection and closing, and the roof needs to be re-inspected
- Buyer loses their job so their loan is denied

Some things are just beyond anyone's control so there is no point in worrying about the improbable things that can go wrong. Resolving these issues takes a great deal of communication and some compromise, and levelheaded real estate professionals on both sides. Do your part and more than likely, everything will work out in the end.

Final Thoughts

There you have it! What you need to know about buying a home. Yes, it is complicated and sometimes stressful, but it is worth the time you invested in reading this book to educate and protect yourself.

Start by hiring a great agent to represent you, and do not ever sign anything until you have a thorough understanding of your risks, responsibilities, and your rights. Don't be a lazy buyer! Ask for help if there is something you don't understand; you can email me at any time with questions that you may have.

Most of all, know that before long you will be moving into your new home, and the stress of the homebuying process will be long forgotten. You will be putting down roots and becoming part of a new community. Many, many firsts will take place in your new home, and countless memories will be created.

My hope is that I have been able to help you avoid the horrible, gut wrenching, stress inducing process that buying a home can be, and that you will have many years of happiness in your new home.

Alysse Musgrave
Exclusive Buyer Broker
Help@HelpUBuyAmerica.com

Made in the USA
Charleston, SC
28 November 2013